Cambridge Elements ≡

Elements in Research Methods for Developmental Science
edited by
Brett Laursen
Florida Atlantic University

IDENTIFYING AND MINIMIZING MEASUREMENT INVARIANCE AMONG INTERSECTIONAL GROUPS

The Alignment Method Applied to Multi-category Items

Rachel A. Gordon
Northern Illinois University

Tianxiu Wang
University of Pittsburgh

Hai Nguyen
University of Illinois at Chicago

Ariel M. Aloe
University of Iowa

CAMBRIDGE
UNIVERSITY PRESS

CAMBRIDGE
UNIVERSITY PRESS

Shaftesbury Road, Cambridge CB2 8EA, United Kingdom

One Liberty Plaza, 20th Floor, New York, NY 10006, USA

477 Williamstown Road, Port Melbourne, VIC 3207, Australia

314–321, 3rd Floor, Plot 3, Splendor Forum, Jasola District Centre, New Delhi – 110025, India

103 Penang Road, #05–06/07, Visioncrest Commercial, Singapore 238467

Cambridge University Press is part of Cambridge University Press & Assessment, a department of the University of Cambridge.

We share the University's mission to contribute to society through the pursuit of education, learning and research at the highest international levels of excellence.

www.cambridge.org
Information on this title: www.cambridge.org/9781009357746

DOI: 10.1017/9781009357784

First published 2023

A catalogue record for this publication is available from the British Library.

ISBN 978-1-009-35774-6 Paperback
ISSN 2632-9964 (online)
ISSN 2632-9956 (print)

Additional resources for this publication at www.cambridge.org/gordon_resources

Identifying and Minimizing Measurement Invariance among Intersectional Groups

The Alignment Method Applied to Multi-category Items

Elements in Research Methods for Developmental Science

DOI: 10.1017/9781009357784
First published online: June 2023

Rachel A. Gordon
Northern Illinois University

Tianxiu Wang
University of Pittsburgh

Hai Nguyen
University of Illinois at Chicago

Ariel M. Aloe
University of Iowa

Author for correspondence: Rachel A. Gordon, rgordon@niu.edu

Abstract: This Element demonstrates how and why the alignment method can advance measurement fairness in developmental science. It explains its application to multi-category items in an accessible way, offering sample code and demonstrating an R package that facilitates interpretation of such items' multiple thresholds. It features the implications for group mean differences when differences in the thresholds between categories are ignored because items are treated as continuous, using an example of intersectional groups defined by assigned sex and race/ethnicity. It demonstrates the interpretation of item-level partial non-invariance results and their implications for group-level differences and encourages substantive theorizing regarding measurement fairness.

Keywords: measurement fairness, measurement invariance, alignment method, intersectionality, children's behavior, socio-emotional development

ISBNs: 9781009357746 (PB), 9781009357784 (OC)
ISSNs: 2632-9964 (online), 2632-9956 (print)

Contents

Online appendices and additional resources for this
publication at www.cambridge.org/gordon_resources

1 Introduction

Psychological measures, tests, and assessments are ubiquitous in many societies (Oakland et al., 2016; Zlatkin-Troitschanskaia et al., 2018). One widespread use has been for tracking academic progress. In the United States, scores on standardized tests contribute to progression to the next grade level and decisions about admission to college as well as to rankings of schools and evaluations of teachers (Lemann, 2000; Moss et al., 2005; Young, 2021). Similar uses in England include standardized testing in primary grades, high-stakes examinations at the end of secondary school, and publicly available rating systems (Rimfeld et al., 2019; Santori, 2020). In China, a tradition of examinations extends back centuries, and contemporary National College Entrance Examinations determine college entry (Bodenhorn et al., 2020; Rotberg, 2010). Beyond testing academic progress, school psychologists also use assessments of social, behavioral, and emotional behaviors to screen children for referrals to intervention in countries around the world (Oakland et al., 2016). And, these school-based usages intersect with clinical and organizational psychology use of tests, as a component of diagnoses of psychiatrically defined disorders and of workplace hiring and promoting (Benjamin, 2005; Rothstein & Goffin, 2006).

Measures, tests, and assessments address the challenge that many key concepts are not directly observable in the psychological sciences, and related social, health, and educational sciences (i.e., are *latent*). It is therefore common to measure latent constructs using things that are observable, such as a series of questions about knowledge, behaviors, expressions, and attitudes that individuals can report. For instance, the Aggression Questionnaire measures individuals' tendencies toward aggression through their answering on a five-point scale how characteristic of them (labeled extremely uncharacteristic, uncharacteristic, neither characteristic nor uncharacteristic, characteristic, and extremely characteristic) are a few dozen actions such as "I flare up quickly but get over it quickly" and "If somebody hits me, I hit back" (Buss & Perry, 1992; Buss & Warren, 2000). As another example, the Achenbach System of Empirically Based Assessment (ASEBA, n.d.) includes versions that ask parents, teachers, and children to report about children's behaviors. Responses to various subsets of items contribute to summary scores in relation to empirically based syndromes and psychiatric diagnostic classifications – for example, contributing to scores on an aggressive behavior syndrome for young children are statements like "Easily frustrated," "Doesn't seem to feel guilty after misbehaving" and "Physically attacks people" which are reported as being not true, somewhat/sometimes true, or very/often true of the child.

Because of the ways such measures gatekeep access to opportunities and mark individuals with prestigious or stigmatizing statuses, their use has been contested (Lemann, 2000; Moss et al., 2005; Young, 2021). Social movements in the 1960s, for instance, heightened attention to the question of whether measures fairly assessed abilities across groups, such as between those who were assigned as female versus male or as Black versus White (Byrne et al., 2009; Davidov et al., 2014). Considerations of fairness addressed questions such as: Do various groups define a construct in the same way? Do the groups view similar knowledge, behaviors, expressions, and attitudes as reflective of the construct? Do groups vary in how they interpret or report about a particular expression or behavior? Continuing the example of tendencies toward aggression introduced earlier, considerations of fairness might include asking whether some groups interpret aggressive conduct as reflecting a behavioral disorder and others do not – for example, would some groups view hitting someone back after being hit as reflective of such a disorder, and other groups consider such a response as a reasonable defense of self? Considerations of fairness might also concern what has been termed *social desirability bias* – the tendency for a person to adjust their responses to be in line with what the person thinks is the expected answer (Duckworth & Yeager, 2015). In other words, for some individuals and some contexts, affirmation of the statement "If somebody hits me, I hit back" might be viewed as a sign of strength, and thus potentially overreported (i.e., endorsed by some people who do not actually hit back when hit), and for others such affirmation might be seen as a weakness and thus potentially underreported (i.e., not endorsed by some people who do actually hit back when hit).

Such complexities in how concepts are defined and interpreted and controversies about how tests are used have led psychometricians to expand strategies for assessing fairness, including the central concept of *measurement invariance* (also known as a *lack of measurement bias*; AERA/APA/NCME, 2014; Camilli, 2006; Xi, 2010). Formally defined in subsequent paragraphs, measurement invariance broadly entails the degree to which a measure's questions operate similarly across groups. As early twenty-first century societies again contend with systemic inequities, and movements call for equity and antiracism, the need is urgent for psychologists to comprehensively consider measurement invariance (Han et al., 2019).

Despite the need for examining measurement invariance as an aspect of fairness, the capacity of the field to do so is limited. Partly the limited field capacity reflects minimal training of students and scholars in psychometrics, and particularly item response theory (IRT) approaches. Over a decade ago, a national survey of graduate programs in psychology in the United States, for instance, found that two-fifths offered no training in IRT and less than one in ten offered full coverage (Aiken et al., 2008). A Canadian survey likewise found few offerings in advanced statistics, including structural equation modeling (Golinski & Cribbie, 2009). Limited coverage was again identified in a recent US national survey that found nearly one quarter of graduate programs completely lacked coverage of psychometrics in introductory statistics courses and another fifth restricted coverage to a single class period or less (Sestir et al., 2021). The consequences of limited field capacity are amplified by the complexity of early strategies for empirically identifying measurement invariance. Iterative approaches for measurement invariance testing are particularly labor intensive, especially when groups are numerous (Cheung & Lau, 2012). Implementing these approaches therefore required particularly advanced levels of programming skill. And, substantive scholars required basic understanding of the techniques in order to best understand the rationale for such investment of time and effort and in order to draw inferences for theory and practice from the volumes of results.

These challenges may contribute to the relative lack of publications documenting invariance for measures commonly used in psychology. For instance, in a large-scale analysis of fifteen widely used measures in social and personality psychology (such as the Rosenberg Self-Esteem Scale), whereas nearly all measures demonstrated good evidence of internal consistency, only one demonstrated good evidence of measurement invariance (Hussey & Hughes, 2020). A review of a representative sample of articles from the *Journal of Personality and Social Psychology* also revealed that the majority of articles reported only reliability coefficients as structural validity evidence; the review authors noted that although they "observed numerous studies which tested hypotheses about numerous populations (e.g., age-groups, cultures) . . . only one tested measurement invariance" (Flake et al., 2017).

The purpose of this tutorial is to support developmental scientists in using and interpreting one recently developed technique for empirically identifying measurement invariance and adjusting for the invariance that is revealed, the *alignment method* (Asparouhov & Muthén, 2014, 2023; Muthén & Asparouhov, 2014). The alignment method was developed for cross-national research (Asparouhov & Muthén, 2014; Marsh et al., 2018; Muthén & Asparouhov, 2014), and has been applied more extensively in that field than in other areas of psychology (e.g., Bansal et al., 2022; Bordovsky et al., 2019; Bratt et al., 2018; Gordon et al., 2022; Lansford et al., 2021; Rescorla et al., 2020). The alignment method differs from other measurement invariance techniques in making it straightforward to allow for *partial invariance* in which some questions similarly reflect a construct across groups and other questions differ in their relationship to the construct across groups. Other measurement invariance techniques have been designed to detect whether invariance holds or not, and offer less guidance or require more complicated strategies when invariance is rejected.

We not only provide an accessible introduction to the key concepts undergirding the alignment method but we also: (a) show how to implement it in the software package *Mplus* using algorithms written by the alignment approach's authors, (b) provide an R package for reading the volumes of results (openly accessible through *GitHub*), and (c) detail how to interpret the results. Importantly, our focus is on the kinds of multi-category (e.g., Likert, 1932) questions common in psychology (such as the five- and three-category response options in the examples of measuring tendencies toward aggression provided earlier). In contrast, existing tutorials and applications of the alignment method have primarily focused on continuous and dichotomous items (e.g., Sirganci et al., 2020). We also differ from prior coverage of the alignment approach with categorical items (e.g., Svetina et al., 2020) in demonstrating how to convert the results to probability units. Probability units help make the results meaningful to substantive scholars and broader stakeholders. In other words, percentages are familiar to many given widespread use, whereas a model coefficient (such as a logit) may be less familiar. In the context of measurement invariance, a difference of 50 to 30 percent may be seen as large, whereas a difference of 41 to 39 percent may be seen as small, when comparing the chances that members of one group versus another would be rated to have "hitting back" behavior be extremely characteristic of them, despite being estimated to have equal latent tendency toward aggression. To illustrate how to implement the alignment method and interpret its results, we offer an empirical example, with code and data available in supplementary materials. Before considering this empirical example, we begin with a conceptual introduction to measurement invariance followed by a formal presentation of central mathematical models.

1.1 Introduction to Measurement Fairness

Much has been written about fairness in measurement, including from those contesting historical uses of standardized testing, from those suggesting ways to conceptualize cross-cultural variations in concepts and their measurement, and from those proposing specific strategies to psychometrically test for invariance and to address its absence (Dorans & Cook, 2016; Hui & Triandis, 1985; Johnson & Geisinger, 2022; Moss, 2016). In this section, we introduce a portion of these writings relevant to understanding the alignment method. Given the limited training in psychometrics across the field of psychology reviewed earlier, we start with a general introduction to concepts of measurement and then discuss the importance of considering intersectionality and categorical items when testing for measurement invariance.

1.1.1 General Measurement Concepts

Similar to regression models allowing psychologists to see if empirical evidence is consistent with theoretical expectations about how one construct relates to another, psychometric models allow psychologists to see if empirical evidence is consistent with theoretical expectations about which knowledge, behaviors, expressions, and attitudes reflect a latent construct. Different from the core fundamentals of regression modeling, however, terminology and epistemology vary considerably across the psychometric literature. In the limited space of a tutorial, we are selective in what we cover.

One way we are selective is related to terminology, where we prioritize the term *measure* whenever possible as we are discussing concepts and offering interpretations. Some psychometric writing instead uses the terms *tests* or *assessments*. Likewise, we aim to use the term *questions* whenever possible to encompass what are sometimes referred to as *items* or *prompts*. One reason for our prioritization of the terms measure and question is to avoid implying that the alignment method can only be used with standardized or academic tests and assessments. Another reason is that we find the terms measure and question can be received by some audiences as more neutral. In contrast, the terms test and assessment can call to mind uses that are high stakes or that imply universally defined and expressed constructs. When introducing terminology and discussing mathematical models, however, we use the words test and item when doing so reflects conventions (e.g., item response theory; differential item functioning, item-level invariance). Here, our goal is to make this tutorial accessible to those already familiar with these conventional terms and to make the cited references accessible to those who want to learn more after reading the tutorial. Even as we do so, we encourage continued reflection and renaming in the field to prioritize inclusivity of terminology.

Another way we are selective in the context of the tutorial is in our focus on measurement invariance in general and the alignment method in particular. This focus allows us to limit our presentation to a set of concepts and techniques that can be covered within space constraints. At the same time, this focus can place out of sight the ways in which testing for measurement invariance is one aspect of a broader project of continuous measure improvement. We thus emphasize that we do in fact see measurement invariance testing as one component of an iterative process of accumulating and considering multiple pieces of evidence before any particular use of a measure. This process may include evidence provided by a measure's developers, yet would also include evidence in the local use context and sharing of ownership, data, and interpretations with an array of stakeholders, including those responding to the measure and those impacted by its scores. Such consideration of local evidence and inclusion of an array of stakeholders are central components of fairness in general, and are relevant to considerations of measurement invariance in particular. The need to revisit the evidence for each potential use reflects the reality that the groups relevant to consider in relation to measurement invariance will differ across applications, and those being measured and impacted by scores will have insights into the meaning of constructs and their expressions. This inclusivity is especially important in fields where measures were historically developed by and with persons of limited diversity, and a critical gaze can illuminate areas of historical bias in the field itself and opportunities for future equity.

With such a critical gaze, we can draw from the body of psychometric models and writings to be part of a more inclusive approach, while recognizing historical biases. The field of psychometrics has itself evolved over time in understanding, reflecting, and changing its approach to fairness. As an example, the Standards for Educational and Psychological Testing, published collaboratively by the American Psychological Association along with the major educational and measurement societies (AERA/APA/NCME, 2014), reflects the latest in a series of publications dating back to the 1950s. The most recent standards elevated fairness as a "fundamental validity issue" that is an "overriding foundational concern" with a central issue being "equivalence of the construct being assessed" across groups (p. 49). This fundamental nature of fairness is in contrast to the prior standards, published in 1999, which limited fairness to specific populations (e.g., persons with disabilities, English language learners; Johnson & Geisinger, 2022).

The latest standards also embrace a unified validity framework (Messick, 1989). What had been seen as distinct types of validity (e.g., content, criterion, consequential) are now recognized as multiple pieces of validity evidence that are brought together when making a decision about whether a measure is suitable for a particular use. Fairness in general, and measurement invariance in particular, can be seen as one aspect of this body of validity evidence. The body of validity evidence is also now seen as continually accumulating, rather than static at the time a test was published. The latest standards advise decision-makers to use a range of strategies, including various psychometric models, as they make a determination regarding the extent to which the full body of evidence supports a proposed use for a measure. In other words, whereas historically a decisionmaker might have cited internal consistency reliability or factor analyses reported in a publisher's manual, contemporary decision-makers would be encouraged to either locate evidence of validity for their specific use or, if none was available, to build such evidence. This evidence would include demonstrating that the measure's questions demonstrated measurement invariance across the relevant groups and in the local context of a specific application.

Tests of measurement invariance in general, and the alignment method in particular, thus offer empirical evidence related to a measure's validity. Results from testing measurement invariance, including with the alignment method, can be combined with other aspects of validity evidence to inform conclusions about multiple aspects of measurement fairness (Byrne et al., 2009; Davidov et al., 2014). At a conceptual level, if the alignment method indicated very little evidence of measurement invariance, decisionmakers might want to reconsider whether and how the construct is defined across groups. If partial invariance was identified, the instances of non-invariance might be probed to consider whether groups differed in terms of what knowledge, behaviors, expressions, or attitudes were reflective of varying levels of the construct. This probing might include how group members interpret the measure's questions that demonstrate non-invariance. This probing might also include considering the extent to which their responses are affected by social stereotypes and norms related to the measured construct. And, this probing might include considering whether the context in which the measure is administered heightens aspects of social desirability.

Strategies to use might include those from the field of measurement theory and practice for using psychometric model results to iteratively improve measures, including by engaging substantive experts to precisely define constructs and to write questions to reflect those constructs (Boulkedid et al., 2011; Evers et al., 2013; Lane et al., 2016; Wolfe & Smith, 2007a, 2007b). Examining patterns of results, in dialogue with diverse stakeholders and informed by scientific and indigenous concepts, literatures, and practices can lead to tentative interpretations (Chilisa, 2020; Sablan, 2019; Sprague, 2016; Walter & Andersen, 2016). Such tentative interpretations might be examined through future revisions of the measure. Complementary methods such as cognitive interviewing, item reviews, and focus groups can also inform interpretations. Throughout this process, collaborators may see that many aspects of measurement fairness are interrelated, as scrutinizing a measure's questions may lead to revised understandings of concepts, and altered definitions of concepts may result in updating a measure's questions. Engaging a range of stakeholders and variety of methods supports iterative and continuous improvement, including representatives from those being measured as well as content and methods experts, all inclusive of the groups being assessed.

As an example, we collaborated with a school district to iteratively improve a measure of students' social-emotional competencies using psychometric approaches including the alignment method. The school district engaged students, teachers, principals, and other stakeholders in interpreting the results. In a Student Voice Data Summit, for instance, students thought different patterns of socialization influenced why high school boys were more likely to endorse a question about "staying calm when stressed" as easy to do compared to high school girls, believing that boys were less likely to admit feeling stress compared to girls, who were more often socially encouraged to discuss their emotions freely. Following findings indicating measurement non-invariance between students who identified as Latino and Latina, the district's research and practice teams partnered on a project to adapt lessons in their social-emotional learning curriculum based on the findings (Gordon & Davidson, 2022).

1.1.2 Importance of Considering Group Intersections

A limitation in historical considerations of measurement fairness, including in psychology, has been a focus on a small number of groups. Indeed, early methods and tutorials often assumed two groups, one focal and one reference (Finch, 2016). With the critical gaze discussed previously, this approach can be seen as problematic, by assuming a binary and privileging one group as focal and othering the second reference group. Cross-national research in contrast more often considered measurement invariance across many groups. The alignment method arose in the latter context, designed to facilitate empirical identification and adjustment of measurement invariance with many groups. Although this cross-national application still tended to consider groups of a single type (multiple nations), the alignment method can be further extended to consider groups defined by layering together multiple aspects of identities, what we refer to as *multilayered groups*.

One way to define such multilayered groups would be to cross-classify multiple variables. If an existing data source had classifications of sex (e.g., male, female) and race-ethnicity (e.g., Black, White, Asian, Latino/a), then eight multilayered groups might be defined (i.e., Black male, Black female, White male, White female, Asian male, Asian female, Latino, Latina), for instance. Groups could also be defined in flexible ways, such as if some participants preferred to label their own identities or to not use labels, including those identifying as queer, nonbinary, or fluid. And, groups could be defined using theoretical paradigms that consider how systems of power intersect in ways that may amplify, mute, or transform one another dynamically, as in the concept of intersectionality (Crenshaw, 1989). By facilitating this flexibility, the alignment methods might be used by scholars to interrogate measurement fairness from a range of theoretical perspectives and incorporate social-justice oriented modern data science, (Covarrubias & Vélez, 2013; Garcia et al., 2018; Sablan, 2019). To achieve larger sample sizes in various groups of interest, integrative analyses of multiple datasets might be used (Fujimoto et al., 2018).

1.1.3 Importance of Accounting for Multi-Category Items

Many psychological measures include questions that have multiple categories, such as Likert-type response structures and the five- and three-category response options offered in earlier examples. Yet, similar to the origins of regression modeling, numerous psychometric methods were first developed assuming continuous variables, and psychologists often continue to rely on these methods. We demonstrate how to use the alignment method with multi-category items. Doing so better conforms the model assumptions with the data. Doing so also allows for presentation of results in ways that are meaningful to substantive scholars and to a range of stakeholders: the probabilities of choosing various categories. Doing so additionally reduces the chance of overlooking important aspects of measurement invariance that are revealed in the category probabilities.

Although the statement that psychometric models used should be designed, implemented, and interpreted recognizing the questions' multi-category structure seems obvious, it has been common for scholars and analysts to adopt models designed for continuous items when questions are multi-category (Rhemtulla et al., 2012). Even when models designed for multi-category questions are used, interpretations of the substantive meaning of results can be incomplete (Gordon, 2015; Meitinger et al., 2020; Seddig & Lomazzi, 2019). Analogous to applying regression models designed for continuous versus multi-category outcomes, results can sometimes be robust across specifications (Long, 1997; Long & Freese, 2014). Yet, robustness across specifications should be evaluated in any particular application and not assumed. And, when models appropriate to multi-category outcomes are used, interpretation requires additional steps to convert to substantively meaningful metrics (e.g., probabilities vs. logits; Long, 1997; Long & Freese, 2014).

In other words, when a measure asks individuals to choose among a set of categorical responses to a question, results are meaningful when reported in terms of response probabilities. We might find, for instance, that 60 percent of one group versus 40 percent of another group are predicted to "strongly agree" with a statement, despite both groups being estimated to have the same level of the underlying construct being measured. We could contrast this result with another where, say, the predicted percentages were 51 percent for the first group and 49 percent for the second group. Here, we discuss how the alignment method makes such calculations. Again, our goal is to make it easier to take this step from estimation to interpretation, given the volumes of results produced by the alignment method and given the need to convert results to meaningful metrics. This goal is consistent with implementation science and related strategies for encouraging the adoption of advanced methods (King et al., 2019; Sharpe, 2013). Reporting in meaningful units makes results more accessible to a range of stakeholders, including those being measured and the substantive scholars, practitioners, policymakers, family, peers, and community members who draw inferences from the scores (Gordon & Davidson, 2022; Moss, 2016). In other words, many will be familiar with percentages and probabilities from day-to-day usage, whereas fewer may be familiar with the logits. In line with modern statistical reporting standards, probabilities also allow stakeholders to consider the real-world importance of a difference, beyond its statistical significance.

1.2 Introduction to Psychometric Methods for Testing Measurement Invariance

There are two general types of psychometric models that can accommodate multi-category questions: *item factor analysis* (*IFA*) and *item response theory* (*IRT*; Embretson & Reise, 2000; Liu et al., 2017; Millsap, 2011). Each has been used to test for measurement invariance. The alignment method uses IFA during estimation. The alignment method also allows results to be translated to IRT format. By presenting both approaches, we support readers connecting to their own prior study of one or both of these methods as well as to the related literatures on each method. We also demonstrate the ways in which each tradition offers insights into measurement invariance.

1.2.1 Review of General Concepts of Item Factor Analysis and Item Response Theory

Psychometric models generally aim to produce empirical evidence regarding the extent to which responses to a measure's set of questions are consistent with the presence of the proposed latent construct. Many psychologists will be familiar with factor analysis, although likely with its most typical presentation assuming continuous items. Here, *factor loadings* are often of focus, capturing the strength of the association between the item and the latent construct. Underlying the factor analytic model are a series of regressions of the continuous item responses on the latent construct, with the loadings being the regression coefficient and a *factor intercept* also being present. As we formalize in the next section, IFA uses a similar formulation, although when items are recognized as having multiple categories (as opposed to being continuous), there are multiple *factor thresholds* rather than a single intercept. The specification we feature is analogous to ordinal logistic regression, which may be familiar to some readers. Just as ordinal logistic regression can produce predicted probabilities for each level of a categorical outcome variable, so too can IFA predict the probabilities of a respondent choosing each category of a multi-category item.

As we show next, the specification we focus upon is also mathematically equivalent between IRT and IFA formulations – that is, the *graded response model* applied to items in which participants can choose one and only one response from a presented set of categories designed to reflect an ordinal progression (Samejima, 1969, 1996, 2010). What differs between the IRT and IFA formulations is how the focal parameters are defined. IRT defines *item discriminations* (rather than the factor loadings of IFA) and *item difficulties* (rather than the factor intercepts/thresholds of IFA). We provide the standard formulas that allow for calculation of item discriminations from factor loadings and the calculation of item difficulties from factor intercepts/thresholds. Despite the mathematical equivalence of IRT and IFA models, they developed separately, and there is considerable terminology unique to each. Within IRT, it is also the case that numerous subliteratures exist, and various writers adopt different terminology. We introduce a subset of the terms most relevant to understanding measurement invariance (see Nering & Ostini, 2010, for comprehensive coverage and cross-walking of terminologies across psychometric models for multi-category items).

Both IRT and IFA models can produce *summary scores* that differ from a traditional approach of simply summing or averaging item responses. Doing so is important both for accurately estimating group differences on the contrasts and for conveying results to stakeholders. In terms of accuracy of estimation, under IRT and IFA, summary scores are the estimated locations on the latent construct of the people being measured, often in a log-odds (logit) metric. One advantage of the logit-metric estimates is that they are on an interval scale, thus well meeting the assumptions for calculating statistics such as means, standard deviations, and regression coefficients. In contrast, the spacing between an items' categories is unknown. The labels of a question's categories typically imply ordinality (e.g., very uncharacteristic, uncharacteristic, neither characteristic nor uncharacteristic, etc.), yet respondents may interpret categories in ways that differ from ordinality and, even when used in an ordinal fashion, the distances between adjacent categories can vary. Psychometric models can test for and reveal such usages, and estimate placement on a latent interval scale. Doing so increases precision of estimation and statistical power.

The person location estimates in a logit metric can also be readily compared to estimates of the latent locations of the items being used to measure the people, which are calculated to be on the same scale. Comparisons between person locations and item locations can facilitate interpretation, including by displaying results graphically to a wide range of stakeholders (Crowder et al., 2019; Morrell et al., 2017). For instance, graphs can reveal when questions tend to fall above or below the latent locations of a sample's respondents – in common parlance, when questions tend to be "hard" or "easy" for sample members. And, graphs can reveal whether questions tend to be spread out along the latent construct, or concentrated in certain regions. In our work with school districts in assessing students' social-emotional competencies, we have used such graphs to help stakeholders think about where questions might need to be added to better distinguish among students of different competency levels. Practitioners resonated with an analogy to a ruler. For instance, we found initially that many items fell below a set of students' competency levels, indicating that most students endorsed all of the competencies asked about in the set of questions, but few items fell in a range that would well differentiate among students in terms of competency level. We looked to the district's standards for social-emotional competency at higher grade levels, and used focus groups with students and teachers, in an effort to develop items spread across the higher levels of competency (Gordon & Davidson, 2022).

We have also found that various stakeholders resonate with viewing the results in terms of the probabilities of choosing the response categories of a multi-category item. Key to measurement invariance is that such probabilities are predicted for children with the same estimated level of the latent construct. For instance, in the measure of young children's aggressive behaviors noted earlier, we might find that the model predicted for one group of students that teachers had a 0.25 probability of choosing the option of "not true" for the question "Easily frustrated," a probability of 0.40 for the option of "somewhat/ sometimes true," and a probability of 0.35 for the option of "very/often true." These results might be contrasted to those for another group of children being 0.50, 0.30, and 0.20, respectively, despite these students having an estimated level of the latent tendency for aggression equivalent to the first group of students.

Such probabilities are often: (a) first predicted from the model across a range of person locations on the latent construct, and (b) then presented graphically in what are referred to as *category probability curves*. The reason for making calculations at a range of person locations on the latent construct is that we want to interpret the extent to which response probabilities vary across the groups despite focusing on individuals from each group who have the same latent level of the construct. In the example of the item "Easily frustrated," we would use formulas from the model to make the calculations of category probabilities and cumulative probabilities for children estimated to be located at low-, mid-, and high- levels of tendencies toward aggressive behavior. Within any given latent location of persons, the probabilities sum to one across the categories, consistent with our focus on items that allow participants to choose one and only one response.

Sometimes, *cumulative probability curves* are also graphed. Cumulative probabilities sum probabilities across a range of a variable's values. In the models for ordinal (e.g., Likert-type) response structures considered in this manuscript, the range is a set starting with a certain category and then including any category above it (Embretson & Reise, 2000; Samejima, 2010). These cumulative probabilities are featured in some models rather than the individual category probabilities because constraints on the cumulative probabilities can simplify models and ensure that the model's estimates conform with an ordinal assumption.

For a three-category item, there would be three such sets for cumulative probability calculations. For instance, in our previous example of a measure of young children's aggressive behaviors, the individual categories would be 1 = not true, 2 = somewhat/sometimes true, and 3 = very/often true. In the first cumulative set, we would start with category 1 and then also include the two categories above it, leading to the set $P_1 = \{1, 2, 3\}$. This first cumulative set thus includes all three of the individual categories. In the second set, we would start with category 2 and then also include the one category above it, leading to the set $P_2 = \{2, 3\}$. This second cumulative set thus includes the two higher categories. In the third set, we would start with category 3 and there would be no categories above it, leading to the set $P_3 = \{3\}$. This third cumulative set thus includes only the highest category.

To calculate the cumulative probabilities, the probabilities of the individual categories in each set are summed together. Earlier, we offered, for the example of a measure of young children's aggressive behaviors, a 0.25 probability of choosing the first option of "not true," a probability of 0.40 for the second option of "somewhat/sometimes true," and a probability of 0.35 for the third option of "very/often true." We can symbolically represent these individual category probabilities as $p_1 = 0.25, p_2 = 0.40$, and $p_3 = 0.35$. The cumulative probability for the first set of {1,2,3} would then be $P_1 = p_1 + p_2 + p_3 = 0.25 + 0.40 + 0.35 = 1$. Note that for the models featured in this manuscript, the sum of the probabilities for all categories will always be one because participants must choose one and only one response. As a result, this set including all categories is typically not shown in graphs, as its probability would always be one. The cumulative probability for the second set of {2,3} would be $P_2 = p_2 + p_3 = 0.40 + 0.35 = 0.75$. In other words, the probability is 0.75 that a teacher selects either the second or the third category for the example item. The cumulative probability for the third set of {3} would be $P_3 = p_3 = 0.35$. This cumulative probability for the highest category is often graphed, although it's helpful to keep in mind that the highest category's cumulative probability curve will be the same as its individual category probability curve. And, of course, the greater the number of categories, the more cumulative probability curves there are between the curve for the lowest and highest values. In other words, whereas for the example of a three-category response structure, there was only one "middle" category, there would be five "middle" categories for a seven-category response structure.

1.2.2 Conventional Strategies to Empirically Identify Measurement Invariance

Before turning to the alignment method in the next section, we introduce conventional strategies for empirically identifying measurement invariance and estimating its substantive size, both with the IFA and the IRT frameworks. We do so because the alignment method shares some terminology with these approaches and uses some of the conventional models as a starting point. Each of the IFA and IRT approaches to measurement invariance allows us to examine the core fairness question of whether response probabilities are statistically equivalent across groups within levels of the latent construct. However, each uses somewhat different terminologies and approaches.

Item Factor Analysis. In factor analysis, the term *measurement invariance* is common, here meaning that the factor loadings and intercepts/thresholds are statistically equivalent across groups (Millsap, 2011). A standard approach to examining *model-level measurement invariance* under the IFA framework has emerged that involves estimating a series of nested models. The *configural model* allows each group to have its own estimates, including of the factor loadings and thresholds for every item. The *metric model* constrains the loadings to be equal across groups for all items, but allows thresholds to be freely estimated for each group on each item. The *scalar model* constrains both the loadings and the thresholds to be equal across groups for every item. If the metric or scalar models show meaningfully worse fit (in ways illustrated herein), then model-level invariance is rejected, referred to as *measurement non-invariance* (Millsap, 2011). Estimating group-specific models such as these is often referred to as *multi-group confirmatory factor analysis*.

In situations of non-invariance, the next step would be to probe *item-level measurement invariance* to see which parameters (loadings, intercepts/thresholds) differ for which groups on which items. If a subset of items' parameters is invariant across groups, then a *partially invariant* model might be specified (Byrne et al., 1989). The advantage of this partially invariant model is that scale scores can be linked across groups through the items that operate equivalently across groups. At the same time, other items' parameter estimates are allowed to differ across groups. No single approach to establishing partial invariance under the IFA framework has achieved consensus as preferred, however. One iterative strategy involves first estimating a metric or scalar model and then using modification indices (expected changes in model fit) in order to choose a first parameter to free (i.e., to allow its value to differ across groups). The parameter selected to be freed has the largest modification index. The process is repeated iteratively until a good fitting model is established. Criticisms of this approach, and other multi-step processes with numerous decision points include: (a) the approaches become unwieldy with many groups and many items, (b) the selected model may not be unique in the current sample (if any judgment is needed in selecting among similar modification indices), and (c) the selected model may be best fitting for the particular sample but not likely to replicate across other samples (Cheung & Lau, 2012).

Item Response Theory. Numerous IRT approaches have also been developed that focus on item-level invariance testing, referred to as empirical tests of *differential item functioning* (*DIF*; Osterlind & Everson, 2009). Although akin to the spirit of IFA tests of measurement-invariance, the traditions producing IRT-based DIF tests used a different logic. First, persons from different groups (e.g., usually two, such as those assigned as female and those assigned as male) but with equivalent levels of the latent construct were identified. Second, within each set of individuals sharing the same level of the latent construct, item response probabilities were compared between the groups (e.g., between those assigned as female and male, among the set identified as having a lower level of the latent construct; between those assigned as female and male, among the set identified as having a higher level of the latent construct). A key challenge of these approaches is that the strategy for identifying equivalent levels of the latent construct either requires making assumptions or requires using iterative strategies. For instance, sometimes all but one of the items are assumed to be DIF-free, so that summary scores based on those items can be used to identify equivalent groups. Then, DIF is tested for the remaining item. If a subset of DIF-free items can be identified, then they are used as *anchors* in a model that allows the remaining items to have their own parameters across groups. Estimating a model anchored in this way is often referred to as *concurrent calibration*, with the anchor items serving as the link putting scores on the same scale across the groups (Kolen & Brennan, 2014). As in the example of individuals assigned as female and male, it is also the case that early tests for DIF assumed two groups, treating one as reference and one as focal, whereas psychologists may be interested in numerous groups (potentially defined by the intersection of multiple variables) and may be interested in all of the pairwise comparisons among these groups (including to avoid privileging one group over another).

Substantive Size. The final topic we introduce from conventional approaches to testing measurement invariance is strategies to calculate the *substantive size* of identified differences (Meade, 2010). In other words, substantive size would be larger if the difference in predictive probabilities was 0.20 points (0.60 vs. 0.40) in comparison to 0.02 points (0.51 vs. 0.49). Although there is no single agreed upon strategy for doing so, some assessment of substantive size should be a priority given the complexity of statistical power in the measurement non-invariance context. Whereas model-level tests of measurement invariance have been found to be underpowered when sample sizes are not balanced across groups (Yoon & Lai, 2018), item-level approaches are often vulnerable to accumulation of Type I error across numerous tests within a single estimation and across iterative estimations. Scholars have also debated whether item-level invariance matters if groups do not differ statistically in their average measure-level scores. This situation can occur if item-level invariance is offsetting across groups. In other words, on some items, members of Group A may have higher probabilities of choosing higher response options than Group B, despite equivalent latent construct levels; yet, on other items, the reverse may be true. Later, we illustrate one approach for considering substantive size at the measure and item levels.

1.3 Introduction to the Alignment Method

The *alignment method* was developed to address limitations of conventional approaches to testing measurement invariance (Asparouhov & Muthén, 2014; Muthén & Asparouhov, 2014). Whereas prior methods focused on two groups, the alignment method allowed many groups. Whereas prior methods required users to implement iterative methods manually, the alignment method's built-in algorithms automated an iterative process. The algorithm also uses a loss function designed to identify an optimal solution, more likely to be replicable. And, the developers programmed the alignment method in Mplus in such a way that many desired results to support interpretation are available in the output. Our R package makes it easy to read the voluminous results produced for measures with categorical questions to present the results in graphical or tabular form, and to make additional calculations.

1.3.1 Nontechnical Description of the Alignment Method

As detailed later, the alignment method relies on an algorithm to identify a set of parameters that minimizes item-level differences across groups. Sets of groups with invariant and non-invariant parameters are identified for each parameter of each item. Then, any such item-level differences across groups are taken into account when group-level means on the latent construct are compared. Although the alignment method estimates the model using IFA, the IFA loadings and thresholds can be translated to the IRT scale of discriminations and difficulties. Predicted probabilities of category responses can also be calculated. Together, the IFA and IRT frameworks allow scholars to draw upon a wide range of established literatures and interpretive strategies.

1.3.2 Nontechnical Description of Strengths and Limitations Relative to Other Approaches

A key strength of the alignment method is that it facilitates identification of a partially invariant solution, with the algorithm programmed in an automated way, avoiding the need for the user to make iterative choices. The benefits of such automation increase as the number of groups (and number of items) increase. The alignment method also can bridge the IFA and IRT traditions. Whereas the alignment method is estimated under the IFA metric, the developers provide equations to translate results to IRT metrics. We have programmed the equations for translation from the IFA to the IRT metric into an R package to facilitate their use. At the same time, the alignment method has limitations. One limitation is that current implementations build specific default criteria into its automated algorithm, such as criteria of $p < 0.01$ and $p < 0.001$ for identifying group differences, discussed shortly. Another limitation is that the alignment method has been implemented to date in Mplus for some but not all types of multi-category models. And, the alignment method is expected to work best when item-level invariance is moderate – that is, found in some but not most items. An approximate limit of 25 percent non-invariance has been suggested to ensure that alignment method results are trustworthy, especially if sample size is small (e.g., $n = 100$ vs. 1000; Muthén & Asparouhov, 2014, p. 3). Although existing simulations suggest the alignment method can identify population-level measurement invariance and well match results from conventional approaches (e.g., Finch, 2016), more work is needed into its algorithmic criteria and assumptions, as we discuss later. The Mplus output from the alignment method is also voluminous, and one objective of this tutorial is to offer strategies to facilitate presentation and interpretation of these results.

One important alternative approach that has been increasingly used by developmental scholars to examine measurement invariance is the multiple-indicator multiple-cause (MIMIC) model and its offshoots, which predict latent variables and their indicators by observed variables (Bauer, 2017; Hauser & Goldberger, 1971). The MIMIC model implements differential item functioning in the context of a structural equation model. For simplicity of the presentation, we consider a single latent variable (i.e., factor) regressed on an observed grouping variable (e.g., sex, male and female) with the goal to estimate group mean differences on the factor. Each item that contributes to the factor is also tested for DIF by regressing the item on the grouping variable (e.g., sex). Differential item function is indicated when group membership significantly predicts item responses in this structural equation modeling context that also accounts for group mean difference at the factor level. There is no consensus in the literature of how MIMIC models should be used to test for DIF. But with some small differences, the common procedure is as follows, similar to the iterative procedure already described for identifying partial invariance (Woods, 2009). First, fit a baseline model assuming no DIF in any item. Then use modification indices to determine if freely estimating a parameter that was fixed would contribute improvement of the model fit. In relation to DIF, items with a "large" modification index for the path between the observed character-istic and the item are flagged. One obvious challenge is how to decide how large a modification index must be. An alternative approach to using modification indices to identify parameters to free is to iteratively test each item for DIF by assuming that all other items are invariant. Under this approach, the baseline model is statistically compared with each one of the subsequent models.

Both the alignment method and the MIMIC model have value, and here we emphasize some reasons why developmental scientists might choose the align-ment method. At one level, the two approaches can be seen as nearly equivalent. As is the case in structural regression models, the explicit definition of *multi-layered groups* defined by their values across several separate variables can, with the appropriate specification, be statistically equivalent to defining inter-actions among the separate variables. Yet, the alignment method is designed in ways that readily accommodate multilayered groups, whereas interactions are more common in the MIMIC models. And, the two approaches vary in what information is foregrounded – the parameters estimated for each unique group (as in the alignment method), or, the significance of differences in parameters among groups (as in the MIMIC model with interactions). Again, the approaches can give equivalent information – differences among group parameters can be tested in the former approach and the multilayered group estimates can be recovered from the interactions. Yet, when three of more separate variables are considered, the numbers of interactions, interpretations of their parameters, and calculations of multilayered groups' estimates become increasingly complex. In other words, a MIMIC model might include a three-way interaction, three two-way interactions, and three terms for the three component variables. If some of the interactions are significant, then postestimation calculations such as simple slopes and predicted values would be needed for interpretation. The results for multilayered groups would be revealed through careful calculation and presentation of such results. In contrast, the separately defined multilayered groups center the identities of the persons forming the groups and retain explicit meaning – for example, Black females living in the rural South of the United States, Black females living in the urban North of the United States. The alignment method not only facilitates elevating these multilayered groups, but also supports getting the kind of information an interaction model would offer, by automating the detection of which groups' estimates are statistically equivalent and statistically different. As we come back to in the discussion, the alignment method still has room for improvement. One of its current limitations is that it allows for only one set of groups with equivalent parameters. Yet, the promise of the alignment method encourages future developments to address this constraint.

Of course, in either the alignment method or a MIMIC model, a limiting factor in defining multilayered groups is sample size. One advantage of the alignment method is that small group sizes are made salient, because the sample size for each group is listed. Some groups defined by multiple characteristics may be clearly too few to support estimation. Limited sample size in certain intersections of separate variables also reduces support for testing interactions, although potentially less saliently (e.g., by noticing standard errors are large, if not explicitly checking the sample sizes in relevant cross-classifications of categorical variables or regions of continuous variables). This relative salience is akin to the way in which propensity score matching makes areas of support and lack thereof more explicit than covariate controls in structural regression models. A limiting factor in the multilayered groups approach is that it is best suited for capturing the intersection of categorical variables. Whereas continuous variables could be categorized, doing so can suffer from the well-recognized loss of information in categorizing continuous variables (Royston et al., 2005). At the same time, when interactions of continuous and categorical variables are examined, nonlinearities in the continuous variables' moderating effect require strategies such as using varying functional forms (i.e., polynomials, splines, or logarithmic transformations). Adding such terms complicates interpretation. Best practice would be to calculate predicted values for each group, because the parameter estimates shown in the output would not directly indicate when one group's estimate falls above or below another group's. For instance, if polynomials were allowed to vary across groups, one group's pattern might be quadratic and another group's cubic. Increasingly complex functional forms may mask areas of small sample size and thus limited support. In other words, the better fit of a quadratic shape relative to a linear shape might be sensitive to a single outlying case that pulls the slope upward. Although it is possible to use careful data screening methods to detect such outliers and to use postestimation calculations to interpret results, some users may find the alignment method easier to implement and interpret given the sample sizes for each multilayered group are directly presented and given output provides both the within-group estimates and the across-group comparisons.

In short, we see the alignment method and MIMIC models as complementary. As psychology and other disciplines encourage attention to replication and robustness of results and related sharing of data and code, the complementary methods can be used within and across research teams. Our goal in the tutorial is to present the alignment method so that more teams can use it in these complementary efforts.

2 Formal Presentation of Psychometric Models

We begin the formal mathematical representation of the *graded response model* using its typical presentation from the IRT framework where it was developed. We then present it with an IFA parameterization, showing how parameters can be translated between the two frameworks. We then cover the *alignment method*, specific to the graded response model. We end with one approach to gauging the substantive size of group differences in item response probabilities, *Raju's signed and unsigned areas*.

2.1 The Graded Response Model: Item Response Theory Parameterization

The common IRT representation of the graded response model's *cumulative probabilities* is

$$P_{ic}(\theta_k) = \frac{\exp[a_i(\theta_k - b_{ij})]}{1 + \exp[a_i(\theta_k - b_{ij})]} = \frac{1}{\exp[-a_i(\theta_k - b_{ij})]}. \tag{1}$$

Notice that the two equivalent equations differ in the sign on a_i. We provide both since each appears in the literature we cite. In the formulas, four indices account for: (a) persons, k; (b) items, i; (c) response categories, c; and (d) the boundaries between adjacent response categories (i.e., difficulties), j. The number of response categories (C_i) equals the number of difficulties (m_i) plus one (i.e., $C_i = m_i + 1$). There is one discrimination parameter per item, a_i. There are m_i *difficulties* for each item. The *cumulative probability*, P_{ic}, is specific to each category of each item and is conditional on θ_k, the location for person k on the latent construct. Notice that the difference between the person location on the latent construct and the difficulty, $\theta_k - b_{ij}$, is a central determinant of the probability. When the person is located above the threshold ($\theta_k - b_{ij} > 0$, the probability will be higher; when the person is located below the threshold ($\theta_k - b_{ij} < 0$), the probability will be lower. In other words, if a person has more of the latent construct than is represented in the difficulty parameter, they will be more likely to choose the higher categories. That the discrimination, a_i, acts as a slope is reflected as it multiplies this difference. Thus, a large discrimination magnifies the difference between the location of the person and the location of the difficulty parameter.

The *category probabilities*, p_{ic}, are calculated by taking the difference between adjacent cumulative probabilities. For instance, when there are three categories, the probability of the middle category would be calculated as $p_2 = P_2 - P_3$. The probability of the lowest category is calculated as $p_1 = 1 - P_2$ (the presence of one in this equation reflects the probability of choosing at least one of the three categories being one, as noted previously). The probability of the highest category is calculated as $p_3 = P_3 - 0$. The presence of zero in this equation reflects there being no categories higher than three (and thus zero probability of choosing such nonexistent categories). The cumulative probabilities can also be calculated as sums of category probabilities (e.g., $P_2 = 1 - p_1 = p_2 + p_3$).

We show in Figure 1 examples of *category probability curves* (top graph) and *cumulative probability curves* (bottom graph), calculated for a range of the latent construct (θ_k) from -3 to 3 and using $a = 1.5$, $b_1 = -1$, and $b_2 = 0$. Recall that the category probability curves show the probabilities of choosing each of an item's categories, conditional of a given latent level of the construct. The latent construct is represented on the x-axis, and the category probabilities sum to one at each level of the latent construct. The cumulative probabilities are sums of category probabilities. The category and cumulative probabilities are identical for the top (third) category. The cumulative probability for the middle (second) category is the sum of the category probabilities for the second and third categories. The cumulative probability for the bottom (first) category is always one (thus not shown in the graph).

Category Probability Curves

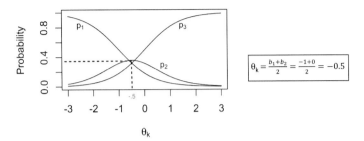

$$\theta_k = \frac{b_1 + b_2}{2} = \frac{-1+0}{2} = -0.5$$

Cumulative Probability Curves

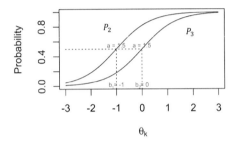

Figure 1 Illustration of Category Probability Curves and Cumulative Probability Curves

Note. The *category probability curves* (top graph) show the probabilities of choosing each of an item's categories, conditional on a given latent level of the construct. The *cumulative probability curves* (bottom graph) are sums of category probabilities. In the graphs, the probabilities are calculated using Equation 1 for a range of the latent construct (θ_k) from -3 to 3 and using $a = 1.5$, $b_1 = -1$, and $b_2 = 0$. The latent construct is represented on the x-axis, and the category probabilities sum to one at each level of the latent construct. The category and cumulative probabilities are identical for the top (3rd) category. The cumulative probability for the middle (2nd) category is the sum of the category probabilities for the 2nd and 3rd categories. The cumulative probability for the bottom (1st) category is always one (thus not shown in the graph).

Beginning with the top graph, notice that the shapes of the three curves are as we would expect for ordinal items. These shapes reflect the graded response model's assumptions of ordinality. That is, the probability of choosing the lowest category (p_1) is high for those with the least amount of the latent construct, θ_k, and then falls off to zero at the highest levels of the latent construct. The probability of the highest category (p_3) follows the reverse pattern. The probability of the middle category (p_2) rises and then falls. As noted earlier, at each level of θ_k (i.e., for persons located at various levels of the latent construct) these three category probabilities sum to one. The item parameters determine the shape and location of the lines. The higher the level of discrimination, the more peaked (narrower and higher) are the middle-category curves and the steeper are the downward and upward slopes of the curves for the lowest and highest categories. For the graded response model, the average of adjacent thresholds determines where the middle categories peak. In Figure 1, the middle category peaks at $\theta = -0.5$ since $\frac{b_1 + b_2}{2} = \frac{-1 + 0}{2} = -0.5$.

In the bottom graph of cumulative probabilities, the curve on the right repeats the curve for the highest category (p_3) from the top graph. The curve on the left is the sum of the middle and highest curves (p_2 and p_3) from the top graph. For both curves, the discrimination parameter, again acts as a slope, determining the steepness of the curves (i.e., higher discriminations reflect steeper slopes). Because each item has a single discrimination parameter, the two curves in the bottom graph have the same shape. The difficulties determine the positioning of these curves, from left to right. If the thresholds are farther apart, then the curves will be more spread out. Specifically, the difficulties, b_{ij}, fall at the level of θ_k at which a person is equally likely to choose the sets of higher versus lower categories. We show this property using dashed lines that cross the y-axis at probability of 0.5 and cross the x-axis at the two difficulty levels (-1 and 0).

2.2 The Graded Response Model: Item Factor Analysis Parameterization

Many readers will be familiar with the standard representation of factor analysis in which a continuous item is regressed upon the latent factor, such as

$$y_i = \nu_i + \lambda_i \eta_k + \epsilon_i,$$

Here, ν_i is the intercept, λ_i is the factor loading, η_k is the latent factor score for a specific individual, and ϵ_i is the residual for the ith item.

For categorical items, multiple thresholds (τ_{ij}) replace the single intercept, being motivated in a way akin to ordinal logistic regression (Long, 1997), whereby someone who would have responded above the threshold on a continuous item chooses the corresponding category of a multi-category item; that is,

$$y_i = \begin{cases} 1, & \text{if } y_i > \tau_{ij} \\ 0, & \text{if } y_i \leq \tau_{ij} \end{cases}.$$

Mplus estimates models with this IFA parameterization, and it is straightforward to calculate the IRT parameters using the following formulas (Asparouhov & Muthén, 2020),

$$a_i = \lambda_i, \tag{3}$$

$$b_{ij} = \frac{\tau_{ij}}{\lambda_i}. \tag{4}$$

The IFA and IRT parameterizations of the graded response model relate as follows,

$$P_{ic}(\theta_k) = \frac{1}{1 + \exp[\tau_{ij} - \lambda_i f_k]} = \frac{1}{\exp[-a_i(\theta_k - b_{ij})]},$$

where $f_k = \alpha + \sqrt{\psi}\theta_k$, and the other parameters are as defined previously. Note that in Eqs. (3) and (4) we have assumed that the factor mean and variance are fixed at zero and one, respectively. In the alignment context, some groups have estimated means and variances. For these groups, our R package relies upon Eqs. (21) and (22) from Asparouhov and Muthén (2020) when converting between IFA and IRT parameterizations. Note also that when the individuals' locations on the latent construct are saved from Mplus' default alignment method specification, the locations will reflect the IFA parameterization rather than the IRT parameterization.

2.3 Statistical Identification of Parameter Estimates

Before turning to the alignment method, we discuss the constraints that must be placed on any IFA and IRT model (including outside of the alignment method context) in order to statistically identify the scale of the latent construct. In doing so, we again emphasize that whereas some psychologists may be used to focusing on factor loadings, with categorical items it is also important to consider the factor intercepts/thresholds. In a multi-group analysis, it is the invariance of these factor intercepts/thresholds that is required to fairly compare the groups' mean levels on the latent variable. Invariance of factor loadings is what is required to fairly consider how the latent variable associates with other variables across groups. For statistical identification purposes, we must therefore consider both means and variances in the distribution of the latent variable.

As in factor analysis with continuous items, recall as well that the reason we need identifying constraints is that the metric of the latent variable is unknown. When modeling the factor means as well as the factor variances, we must establish two aspects of the metric: (a) its *origin*, meaning the starting point of the metric, and (b) its *units*, meaning how much "one more" represents. To set the origin, a parameter is constrained to be zero. To set the units, a parameter is constrained to be one. The constraint of zero is placed either on a latent mean or a threshold/difficulty. The constraint of one is placed either on the latent variance or a loading/discrimination. Although the choice of which parameter to constrain typically produces equivalent results for a single-group IFA or IRT model, the choices of which parameters to constrain have greater implications in the multi-group measurement invariance context. We discuss in the next section how the alignment method achieves statistical identification.

2.4 The Alignment Method

The alignment method's algorithm uses the following general logic. It begins with the *configural model* previously defined for the IFA approach to testing model-level measurement invariance (allowing all groups to have their own loadings and thresholds). The final alignment solution has equivalent fit as this configural model, but the aligned loadings and thresholds as well as the aligned factor means and variances have been adjusted in order to minimize the extent of loading and threshold non-invariance across groups. An iterative alignment process starts by making pairwise contrasts among the configural-model estimated parameters of all groups, and using $p > 0.01$ to "connect" groups (i.e., make an initial determination that they are statistically equivalent; Asparouhov & Muthén, 2014, p. 5). Based on the results, an initial set of groups with statistically equivalent parameters (i.e., invariant groups) is identified. Of note, different sets of invariant groups may be identified for the loading and thresholds of each item. In other words, Item 1 may be estimated to have statistically equivalent loadings, but statistically different first thresholds. In the next steps of the alignment process, the invariant sets are iteratively revised by comparing new estimates to the sample-size weighted average of the parameter estimates for the invariant groups. At this stage, if $p > 0.001$, then a group is added to the invariant set (Asparouhov & Muthén, 2014, p. 5). The process continues until stopping criteria are met. At the final stage, non-invariant groups' estimates differ significantly from the weighted average, whereas invariant groups' estimates do not (Asparouhov & Muthén, 2014; Muthén & Asparouhov, 2014).

More formally, the following equations show how the alignment method transforms the loadings and thresholds from the original configural model at the start of the process (Asparouhov & Muthén, 2014; Muthén & Asparouhov, 2014),

$$\lambda_{ig,1} - \frac{\lambda_{ig,0}}{\sqrt{\psi_g}},$$

$$\nu_{ijg,1} = \nu_{ijg,0} - \alpha_g \frac{\lambda_{ijg,0}}{\sqrt{\psi_g}},$$

where g indexes groups, the original configural estimates have subscript 0, the aligned estimates have subscript 1, and all other terms have been previously defined (for simplicity, here the equations are shown for a single intercept, although the approach can incorporate multiple thresholds). Notice that the loadings, intercepts, factor means, and factor variances are all group specific in these equations (i.e., have subscript g). The alignment method's algorithm uses the following loss function in order to identify the values of the factor means, α_g, and the factor variances, ψ_g, that minimize measurement non-invariance (Muthén & Asparouhov, 2014)

$$F = \sum_i \sum_{g<g'} w_{g,g'} f(\lambda_{ig,1} - \lambda_{ig',1}) + \sum_i \sum_j \sum_{g<g'} w_{g,g'} f(\nu_{ijg,1} - \nu_{ijg',1}),$$

where $w_{g,g'}$ is defined as $\sqrt{N_g N_{g'}}$. In other words, this loss function sums the differences of the loadings and intercepts (thresholds) between groups while weighting by a function of the groups' sample sizes such that larger groups contribute more to the loss function. To make estimation computationally feasible, Asparouhov and Muthén (2014) suggested the following component loss function f:

$$f(x) = \sqrt{\sqrt{x^2 + \kappa}},$$

where κ is a positive small number such as 0.0001.

Identification of the units of the latent scale is achieved through the constraint that the product of the groups' factor variances is one, that is, $\psi_1 \times \ldots \times \psi_g = 1$. This constraint also implicitly links the scale across groups. Mplus uses this constraint during estimation, and then rescales the results to report them with the variance set to one in the first group, $\psi_1 = 1$, and estimated in the remaining groups (Asparouhov & Muthén, 2014, p. 3). The authors of the alignment method assert that this constraint is sufficient to identify all the factor means as well as the factor variance, although they offer two parameterizations for the factor means. We focus on the *fixed* parameterization, whereby the first group's factor mean is fixed to zero. In the *free* parameterization all groups' factor means are estimated (Asparouhov & Muthén, 2014, p. 3). We provide results from the free parameterization in the supplementary materials.

To assess the extent of invariance, Asparouhov and Muthén (2014) proposed an R^2 measure indicating the degree to which variation of each loading and threshold parameter across groups in the configural model was explained by the alignment process. Specifically,

$$R^2_{\nu_j} = 1 - \frac{\mathrm{var}\left(\nu_0 - \nu - \alpha_g \lambda\right)}{\mathrm{var}(\nu_0)}, \text{ and}$$

$$R^2_{\lambda} = 1 - \frac{\mathrm{var}\left(\lambda_0 - \psi_g \lambda\right)}{\mathrm{var}(\lambda_0)},$$

where ν_0 is the intercept of the configural model, λ_0 is the loading of the configural model, ν is the average of the aligned intercepts across all groups, λ is the average of the aligned loadings across all groups, α_g is the aligned mean of the latent variable, ψ_g is the aligned variance of the latent variable, and $R^2_{\nu_j}$ and R^2_{λ} are the R^2 measures for the intercept and loading, respectively (the item subscript is omitted for simplicity of the notation). In the case of multi-category items, the intercept equation is extended for multiple thresholds. This R^2 gives the percentages of variation across groups in each of the configural-parameterized loading and threshold parameters that is explained by variation in the parameter residuals (the configural estimate less a function of the average aligned estimates). The closer the R^2 value is to one, the higher the invariance; the closer the value is to zero, the lower the invariance.

2.5 Substantive Size of Measurement Non-invariance

In IRT, it is common to compare the cumulative probability curves of two groups when assessing DIF (i.e., differential item functioning). Given the cumulative probability curves are conditional on latent levels, as discussed previously, these comparisons can reveal the hallmark of DIF – that two groups have different response probabilities despite equivalent latent levels. When doing so, *uniform* and *nonuniform* DIF are distinguished. Uniform DIF happens when one group's conditional cumulative probability is consistently higher (or consistently lower) than the other group's across the full range of the latent construct. Mathematically, the fact that one group's conditional cumulative probability is consistently higher (or lower) than another group's conditional cumulative probability means that the cumulative probability curves for the two groups are different, but do not cross. Recall that discrimination parameters are analogous to regression slopes. When the slopes are the same between two groups, they do not cross. In such cases, any difference between groups is reflected in their intercepts. For uniform DIF, the discrimination parameters are the same between the groups, and any DIF reflects the difficulties. Conversely, nonuniform DIF occurs when the cumulative probability curves for two groups cross. This means that one group's conditional cumulative probabilities are higher than another group's conditional cumulative probabilities in some of the range of the latent construct, but lower in others. Under nonuniform DIF, differences between groups' conditional cumulative probabilities in one range of the latent construct may cancel out differences between groups' conditional cumulative probabilities in another range of the latent construct, at least to some degree. Nonuniform DIF might lead to minimal differences in the overall means for each group, even though item-level differences could be sizable.

To summarize the magnitude of DIF (i.e., differential item functioning), Raju (1988, 1990) introduced formulas to compute what are referred to as *signed* and *unsigned* areas between cumulative probability curves. These formulas were later extended to polytomous items (e.g., Raju et al., 2009). Signed areas allow for canceling out of positive and negative values. Unsigned areas do not. Differences between the two reflect nonuniform DIF. One way to represent the core aspect of the calculation is (Raju et al., 2009)

$$\sum_{c=1}^{m} p_{ic_A}(\theta_k) Y_{ic} - \sum_{c=1}^{m} p_{ic_B}(\theta_k) Y_{ic}.$$

The calculations rely upon the category probabilities from the *category probability curves*. These probabilities are multiplied by the numbers attached to the response categories (e.g., $Y_{ic} = 1, 2, 3$). The distinct probabilities of the two groups being compared are represented by A and B (e.g., p_{ic_A} for Group A). As a result, each summation provides an expected score for one of the groups. Their difference tells us the extent to which one group's expected score is above or below the other group's. The difference can be interpreted in the scale of the original response categories. The same procedures are used for the unsigned area, with the distinction being that the unsigned area relies upon the absolute values of the differences.

3 Empirical Example

3.1 Dataset and Items

We present an example that draws upon two publicly available datasets, the Children of the National Longitudinal Survey of Youth, 1979 Cohort (CNLSY-79) and the Child Development Supplements of the Panel Study of Income Dynamics (PSID-CDS). From each study, we randomly retained one wave of data for children who were ages 4 to 12 between 1986 and 2016. Both studies asked mothers to rate a focal child's behavior using the Behavior Problems Index (BPI; Parcel & Menaghan,

1988; Zill, 1990). For the empirical example, we focus on six items. Three captured behaviors that the scale labeled as *headstrong* (argues too much; is stubborn, sullen, or irritable; has strong temper and loses it easily). Three captured behaviors that the scale labeled as *hyperactive* (has difficulty concentrating/paying attention; is impulsive or acts without thinking; is restless, overly active, cannot sit still). Each of the six items had three response options: (a) *not true*, (b) *sometimes true*, and (c) *often true*. We defined six groups based on the intersection of assigned sex and race/ethnicity: (a) Latino ($n = 1,112$), (b) non-Latino Black, male ($n = 2,158$), (c) non-Latino White, male ($n = 3,294$), (d) Latina ($n = 977$), (e) non-Latina Black, female ($n = 2,149$), and (f) non-Latina White, female ($n = 3,281$). For ease of reading, and given we will be referencing non-invariance and to avoid the sense of a double negative, we exclude the non-Latina/o prefix in the following sections. The analysis dataset is available in the supplementary materials.

3.2 Multi-group-Confirmatory Factor Analysis Models in Mplus

We first estimated a series of configural, metric, and scalar multi-group confirmatory factor analysis models, and summarize their chi-square, Akaike's Information Criterion (AIC), and Bayesian Information Criterion (BIC) fit statistics in Table 1. We focus on AIC and BIC given the original

Table 1 Fit of Configural, Metric, and Scalar Multi-Group Confirmatory Factor Analysis Models

	Fit Values			
	AIC	**BIC**	**BIC-adj**	**Log-likelihood**
Configural	165200.05	166089.04	165710.87	-82481.03
Metric	165205.69	165945.27	165630.65	-82503.84
Scalar	165746.04	166112.09	165956.38	-82824.02
	Difference in Fit			
	AIC	**BIC**	**BIC-adj**	**Chi-square(df) [*p*-value]**
Metric vs. Configural	5.635	−143.774	−80.216	41.72(20) [.003]
Scalar vs. Configural	**545.988**	**23.055**	**245.508**	**676.17(70) [.000]**
Scalar vs. Metric	**540.353**	**166.829**	**325.724**	**651.58(50) [.000]**

Note. $n = 12,971$. AIC = Akaike's Information Criterion. BIC = Bayesian Information Criterion. BIC-adj is sample size adjusted. Bolded values have difference in AIC and BIC > |10| and *p*-values < .001. All models estimated with robust marginal maximum likelihood (MLR) and a logit link. The alignment method has equivalent fit statistics to the configural model.

implementation of the alignment method under the tradition of maximum likelihood estimation and the historical use of maximum likelihood estimation in IRT modeling and its use in the alignment method (Muthén & Asparouhov, 2014, p. 3). AIC and BIC are also consistent with modern statistical approaches that have moved away from the historical prominence of null hypothesis significance testing, apply across many estimation and model comparison contexts (including least squares and non-nested models), and have guidance for assessing the extent of evidence for further considering models being compared (Burnham & Anderson, 2002; Raftery, 1995). The alignment method has recently been extended to weighted least squares estimation in Mplus (Asparouhov & Muthén, 2023), and we return to the topic of alternative fit indices next.

In our large sample, all three chi-square statistics were significant at the 5 percent level, although only the contrasts with the scalar model had *p*-values <0.001. The fit statistics demonstrate that the metric model – constraining all loadings to be equal across groups but allowing thresholds to be freely estimated across groups – fit about equivalently to the configural model based on AIC (difference in AIC of about 6) and meaningfully better than the configural model based on BIC (about 144 points lower on BIC; about 80 points lower on the adjusted BIC; Burnham & Anderson, 2002; Raftery, 1995). The scalar model – which constrained the thresholds in addition to the loadings to be equal across groups – fit appreciably worse than both the configural and metric models (differences of 23 to 546 points). We next turn to the alignment method for additional item-level evidence regarding whether any of the individual loadings are non-invariant across groups and to identify which thresholds are non-invariant.

3.3 Running the Alignment Method in Mplus

Table 2 presents an example Mplus input file for specifying the alignment method. Much of the code is the same as for a confirmatory factor analysis, and we highlighted in gray three key aspects of the code for the alignment specification. First, the `ALIGNMENT =` subcommand in the `ANALYSIS:` section requests the alignment method. Either the `FIXED` or `FREE` parameterization may be requested. Only the `Configural` model is allowed; its name must be stated in parentheses. Second, alignment relies upon numerical integration, which is requested with `ALGORITHM = INTEGRATION`. Third, the `ALIGN` option in the `OUTPUT:` section requests extra alignment output that is useful for interpretation, as we discuss next. The `Harmony` R package expects that this optional output has been requested (and errors may occur if it has not been requested).

Table 2 Example Mplus Input File for Alignment Method

TITLE:	Alignment (fixed)	! Descriptive title
DATA:	FILE = NLSYPSIDbpi.dat ;	! No path needed if files are in same folder
VARIABLE:	NAMES = subgroup bpi8 bpi10 bpi11 bpi12 bpi14 bpi16 childid ;	! All variables in raw DATA file
	CATEGORICAL = bpi8 bpi10 bpi11 bpi12 bpi14 bpi16 ;	! Categorical items for analysis
	IDVARIABLE = childid ;	! Unique identifier of children
	CLASSES = c(6) ;	! Number of subgroups
	KNOWNCLASS = c(subgroup = 1 2 3 4 5 6) ;	! Variable and values identifying subgroups
ANALYSIS:	TYPE = MIXTURE ;	! Alignment requires MIXTURE type
	ESTIMATOR = MLR ;	! Alignment with categorical items allows ML or MLR
	LINK = LOGIT ;	! Alignment with categorical items allows LOGIT or PROBIT link
	ALIGNMENT = FIXED(Configural) ;	! Alignment can use FIXED or FREE approach ! Alignment only possible with Configural model
	ALGORITHM = INTEGRATION ;	! Alignment relies upon numerical integration
OUTPUT:	ALIGN;	! Requests extra output to be read in by Harmony R package
SAVEDATA:	file is alignment-fixed.txt ;	! Location to save factor scores
	save = fscores ;	! Request factor scores be saved
MODEL:	%OVERALL%	! Describe overall model of a mixed model
	HEADSTRG BY bpi8 ; HEADSTRG BY bpi10 ; HEADSTRG BY bpi11 ;	! Loading of 1st item on Headstrong factor ! Loading of 2nd item on Headstrong factor ! Loading of 3rd item on Headstrong factor
	HYPERACT BY bpi12 ; HYPERACT BY bpi14 ; HYPERACT BY bpi16 ;	! Loading of 1st item on Hyperactive factor ! Loading of 2nd item on Hyperactive factor ! Loading of 3rd item on Hyperactive factor
	HEADSTRG with HYPERACT ;	! Factor covariance

Table 3 displays a summary invariance table included in the Mplus alignment results that lists the name of each loading and threshold alongside numbers representing the groups. Groups that are non-invariant have their numbers enclosed in parentheses. Groups that are invariant have their numbers listed without parentheses. The thresholds are listed first, followed by the loadings. Thresholds are listed within items, with a dollar sign preceding a number to indicate each level. In our case, since we have three response categories, there are two thresholds represented by $1 and $2. For instance, Item 8's second threshold is represented by BPI8$2. We added rectangles around each item's threshold listings for readability, and also placed letters adjacent to some of these rectangles for easy reference.

Substantively, the example shows full invariance for the loadings. No group numbers are enclosed in parentheses for the loadings of each factor's trio of items (the factors being labeled HEADSTRG and HYPERACT). This result reinforces the minimal evidence of metric non-invariance evident in the multi-group confirmatory factor analysis model-level tests of fit. In contrast, four of the six items have partial non-invariance for thresholds, again consistent with the greater evidence for non-invariance evident in the multi-group confirmatory factor analysis results. Two of these items show non-invariance for both thresholds (Items 11 and 14; see letters C and D in Table 3). Two items show non-invariance just for the first threshold (Items 8 and 10; lettered A and B). Looking at which groups are enclosed in parentheses, we see that Group 6 (White females) has the greatest non-invariance (four instances, within three of the four lettered rectangles), followed by Group 3 (White males; two instances, lettered rectangles C and D). All other groups except Latinas have a single instance of non-invariance. Between the two factors, more threshold non-invariance is evident for the items in the Headstrong factor (Items 8, 10, and 11) than the items in the Hyperactive factor (Items 12, 14, and 16).

Altogether, the degree of non-invariance falls below the recommended 25% limit, suggesting that the alignment method results are trustworthy in this application. This trustworthiness was evident overall as well as within parameter types. Specifically, there were 9 non-invariant parameter estimates of 108 across all groups, items, and loadings/thresholds, or 8% overall (i.e., $9/(6 \times 18) = 9/108 = 8\%$) which is below the 25% limit. Within parameter types, no non-invariance was evident for loadings. Nine instances of non-invariance were evident for thresholds, or 12.5% ($9/(6 \times 12) = 12.5\%$), again below the 25% limit. More of the threshold non-invariance was evident at the first threshold, 7 instances, than the second

Table 3 Summary Invariance ("Parentheses") Table from Mplus Alignment Output

APPROXIMATE MEASUREMENT INVARIANCE (NONINVARIANCE) FOR GROUPS

Intercepts/Thresholds

```
BPI8$1     1 (2) 3 4 (5) 6       A
BPI8$2     1 2 3 4 5 6

BPI10$1    1 2 3 4 5 (6)         B
BPI10$2    1 2 3 4 5 6

BPI11$1    (1) 2 (3) 4 5 6       C
BPI11$2    1 2 3 4 5 (6)

BPI12$1    1 2 3 4 5 6
BPI12$2    1 2 3 4 5 6

BPI14$1    1 2 (3) 4 5 (6)       D
BPI14$2    1 2 3 4 5 (6)

BPI16$1    1 2 3 4 5 6
BPI16$2    1 2 3 4 5 6
```

Loadings for HEADSTRG

```
BPI8       1 2 3 4 5 6
BPI10      1 2 3 4 5 6
BPI11      1 2 3 4 5 6
```

Loadings for HYPERACT

```
BPI12      1 2 3 4 5 6
BPI14      1 2 3 4 5 6
BPI16      1 2 3 4 5 6
```

Groups:

1 = Latino
2 = Non-Latino Black, male
3 = Non-Latino White, male
4 = Latina
5 = Non-Latina Black, female
6 = Non-Latina White, female

Items:

BPI8 = argues too much
BPI10 = is stubborn, sullen, or irritable
BPI11 = has strong temper and loses it easily

BPI12 = has difficulty concentrating/paying attention
BPI14 = is impulsive or acts without thinking
BPI16 = is restless, overly active, cannot sit still

Rating Categories:

1 = not true
2 = sometimes true
3 = often true

Factors:

HEADSTRG = headstrong
HYPERACT = hyperactive

Note. Groups lacking parentheses are identified as invariant by the alignment method. Groups enclosed in parentheses are identified as non-invariant for the listed parameter. Thresholds are designated by $1 and $2. Rectangles enclosing each item's thresholds added for readability.

threshold, 2 instances, although both fell below 25% at 19.4% and 5.6%, respectively ($7/(6 \times 6) = 19.4\%$ vs. $2/(6 \times 6) = 5.6\%$).

Given this application meets the criterion of trustworthiness, we move forward with examining which items and parameters are non-invariance. Looking at the results in more detail, for both Item 11 (has strong temper and loses it easily) and Item 14 (is impulsive or acts without thinking) the second threshold is non-invariant for White females (Group 6). For Item 14, non-invariance is also evident on the first threshold for White females; this first threshold is additionally non-invariant for White females for Item 10 (is stubborn, sullen, or irritable). White males (Group 3) also demonstrate non-invariance for the first threshold of Items 11 and 14. Latinos also demonstrate non-invariance for Item 11's first threshold. Finally, Item 8 (argues too much) demonstrates non-invariance on the first threshold for both Black males and Black females. Stopping at such a list of non-invariant parameters for particular items and groups is of little value, including for substantive scholars and practitioners. Thus, we demonstrate next how to use additional results to interpret these instances of non-invariance, including how use of category probabilities calculated by the Harmony package are particularly informative for drawing meaning from the results.

3.3.2 Group-Specific Results in Mplus Alignment Output

Additional Mplus output lists the estimates for each group, along with their standard errors, test statistics, and p-values. Table 4 shows the listings for the first two groups in our example. Although known groups, Mplus lists them as Latent Classes – that is, in our example, Latent Class 1 is Latinos and Latent Class 2 is Black males. Within each group, the factor loadings are listed first. For instance, we first see a header of HEADSTRG BY for the loadings of the three items of the first factor. Then we see a header of HYPERACT BY for the loadings of the three items of the second factor. The factor covariances are listed next (HEADSTRG WITH HYPERACT). The following are the factor means (Means), the item thresholds (Thresholds), and the factor variances (Variances).

In subsequent paragraphs, we will interpret results in more detail. For now, we note that as expected under the FIXED alignment method, the first group's factor means are fixed at zero. The fixing of these parameters is evident not only by the Estimate values being 0.000, but also because the standard errors are listed as 0.000 and the test statistics and p-values are listed as 999.000 (see rectangle A in Table 4). Also, recall that Mplus reports results with a scaling that fixes the factor variances to one in the first group. This constraint is evident in the output, where the variances have corresponding standard errors of 0.000 and test statistics and p-values listed as

Table 4 Group-Specific Results for First Two Groups from Mplus Alignment Output

Latent Class 1 (1)

	Estimate	S.E.	Est./S.E.	Two-Tailed P-Value	
HEADSTRG BY					
BPI8	2.093	0.162	12.916	0.000	
BPI10	2.519	0.221	11.400	0.000	
BPI11	2.224	0.185	12.021	0.000	
HYPERACT BY					
BPI12	1.518	0.138	10.958	0.000	
BPI14	2.190	0.203	10.767	0.000	
BPI16	1.786	0.158	11.318	0.000	
HEADSTRG WITH					
HYPERACT	0.852	0.025	33.458	0.000	[A]
Means					
HEADSTRG	0.000	0.000	999.000	999.000	
HYPERACT	0.000	0.000	999.000	999.000	
Thresholds					
BPI8$1	-0.443	0.102	-4.346	0.000	
BPI8$2	2.942	0.176	16.699	0.000	
BPI10$1	0.499	0.118	4.227	0.000	
BPI10$2	4.691	0.303	15.473	0.000	
BPI11$1	0.591	0.110	5.369	0.000	[F]
BPI11$2	3.906	0.232	16.864	0.000	
BPI12$1	0.185	0.085	2.178	0.029	
BPI12$2	2.783	0.145	19.163	0.000	
BPI14$1	0.307	0.106	2.905	0.004	
BPI14$2	4.335	0.274	15.822	0.000	
BPI16$1	0.147	0.092	1.597	0.110	
BPI16$2	2.763	0.167	16.533	0.000	
Variances					
HEADSTRG	1.000	0.000	999.000	999.000	
HYPERACT	1.000	0.000	999.000	999.000	[B]

Latent Class 2 (2)

	Estimate	S.E.	Est./S.E.	Two-Tailed P-Value	
HEADSTRG BY					
BPI8	1.589	0.166	9.556	0.000	
BPI10	2.582	0.185	13.949	0.000	
BPI11	2.547	0.230	11.075	0.000	
HYPERACT BY					
BPI12	1.634	0.139	11.764	0.000	
BPI14	1.484	0.164	9.043	0.000	
BPI16	1.829	0.155	11.789	0.000	
HEADSTRG WITH					
HYPERACT	0.983	0.124	7.892	0.000	
Means					
HEADSTRG	0.037	0.070	0.526	0.599	
HYPERACT	0.190	0.057	3.369	0.001	[C]
Thresholds					
BPI8$1	0.018	0.120	0.148	0.883	[E]
BPI8$2	2.722	0.138	19.764	0.000	
BPI10$1	0.396	0.174	2.281	0.023	
BPI10$2	4.532	0.240	18.893	0.000	
BPI11$1	0.938	0.180	5.218	0.000	
BPI11$2	4.236	0.239	17.745	0.000	
BPI12$1	0.049	0.092	0.537	0.592	
BPI12$2	3.183	0.134	23.782	0.000	
BPI14$1	0.162	0.091	1.782	0.075	
BPI14$2	3.999	0.166	24.114	0.000	
BPI16$1	0.167	0.094	1.789	0.074	
BPI16$2	3.204	0.158	20.285	0.000	
Variances					
HEADSTRG	1.119	0.182	6.151	0.000	
HYPERACT	1.583	0.274	5.782	0.000	[D]

Note. Groups are listed as latent classes by Mplus, although they are known (i.e., Latent Class 1 = Latino, Latent Class 2 = non-Latino Black male). HEADSTRG = headstrong factor. HYPERACT = hyperactive factor.

999.000 (see rectangle B in Table 4). It is additionally the case that the estimates are not fully standardized, and factor loadings can exceed one.

In contrast, Group 2's factor means and variances are estimated. The mean is slightly (but nonsignificantly) higher than zero for Headstrong ($\hat{\mu}_{12} = 0.037$, $p = 0.599$, where the subscripts 1 and 2 represent the first factor and the second group, respectively) and close to significantly higher for Hyperactive, using $\alpha = 0.001$ ($\hat{\mu}_{22} = 0.190$, $p = 0.001$; see rectangle C in Table 4). The estimated variances are $\hat{\psi}_{12} = 1.119$ and $\hat{\psi}_{22} = 1.583$ (see rectangle D in Table 4). For later reference, we also enclosed in rectangles the first thresholds for Items 8 and 11 which were flagged as non-invariant for Groups 2 and 1, respectively (rectangles E and F).

3.3.3 Detailed Alignment Results in Mplus Output

Table 5 provides detailed results produced by the alignment method. Such results are listed for every parameter (loading and thresholds) for every item. We show examples for the first thresholds of Items 8 (left panel) and 11 (right panel). The output begins with contrasts between each pair of groups. Next, the output lists which groups are invariant and provides the weighted average of the parameter estimated for these invariant groups as well as the proportion of configural variance in that parameter that is explained by the alignment method. Finally, the differences between each invariant group's alignment-estimated value and the invariant weighted average are provided along with the standard error and p-value associated with these differences.

To draw meaning from these results, we begin by comparing them to those shown in Table 3. Notice that the groups with parentheses in Table 3 are complementary to the groups listed as non-invariant in Table 5. In other words, for the first threshold of Item 8, Groups 2 and 5 are enclosed in parentheses in Table 3, and the remaining Groups 1, 3, 4, and 6 are listed as non-invariant in Table 5 (compare rectangles labeled A in Table 3 and labeled C in Table 5). Likewise, for the first threshold of Item 11, Groups 1 and 3 are enclosed in parentheses in Table 3, and the remaining Groups 2, 4, 5, and 6 are listed as non-invariant in Table 5 (compare rectangles labeled C in Table 3 and labeled D in Table 5).

We feature two other aspects of the results in Table 5 (see also Asparouhov & Muthén, 2014, p. 5) to help readers understand how groups are placed into invariant and non-invariant sets across the iterative stages of the alignment method. First, the significance tests relative to the weighted average reflect the ending point of the alignment method. These are the values that determined invariance versus non-invariance, as in the

Table 5 Detailed Invariance Results for the First Threshold of Two Items from Mplus Alignment Output

Intercepts/Thresholds
Threshold 3PI8$1

Group	Group	Value	Value	Difference	SE	P-value	
2	1	0.018	-0.443	0.461	0.139	0.001	A
3	1	-0.709	-0.443	-0.266	0.137	0.053	
3	2	-0.709	0.018	-0.727	0.096	0.000	
4	1	-0.663	-0.443	-0.220	0.170	0.196	
4	2	-0.663	0.018	-0.681	0.137	0.000	
4	3	-0.663	-0.709	0.046	0.117	0.695	
5	1	-0.185	-0.443	0.258	0.149	0.084	
5	2	-0.185	0.018	-0.203	0.103	0.048	
5	3	-0.185	-0.709	0.524	0.095	0.000	
5	4	-0.185	-0.663	0.478	0.135	0.000	
6	1	-0.713	-0.443	-0.270	0.149	0.069	
6	2	-0.713	0.018	-0.731	0.100	0.000	
6	3	-0.713	-0.709	-0.004	0.072	0.956	
6	4	-0.713	-0.663	-0.050	0.117	0.670	
6	5	-0.713	-0.185	-0.528	0.098	0.000	

C Approximate Measurement Invariance Holds For Groups:
1 3 4 6
Weighted Average Value Across Invariant Groups: -0.671 E
R-square/Explained variance/Invariance index: 0.280 J

Invariant Group Values, Difference to Average and Significance

Group	Value	Difference	SE	P-value	
1	-0.443	0.228	0.120	0.058	G
3	-0.709	-0.038	0.040	0.344	
4	-0.663	0.008	0.099	0.934	
6	-0.713	-0.042	0.045	0.353	

Threshold BPI11$1

Group	Group	Value	Value	Difference	SE	P-value	
2	1	0.938	0.591	0.347	0.182	0.056	B
3	1	0.656	0.591	0.065	0.150	0.667	
3	2	0.656	0.938	-0.283	0.112	0.011	
4	1	1.123	0.591	0.532	0.193	0.006	
4	2	1.123	0.938	0.184	0.159	0.245	
4	3	1.123	0.656	0.467	0.140	0.001	
5	1	1.275	0.591	0.684	0.179	0.000	
5	2	1.275	0.938	0.337	0.114	0.003	
5	3	1.275	0.656	0.620	0.097	0.000	
5	4	1.275	1.123	0.152	0.136	0.262	
6	1	1.239	0.591	0.648	0.175	0.000	
6	2	1.239	0.938	0.301	0.131	0.022	
6	3	1.239	0.656	0.583	0.106	0.000	
6	4	1.239	1.123	0.116	0.144	0.421	
6	5	1.239	1.275	-0.036	0.091	0.689	

D Approximate Measurement Invariance Holds For Groups:
2 4 5 6
Weighted Average Value Across Invariant Groups: 1.159 F
R-square/Explained variance/Invariance index: 0.566 I

Invariant Group Values, Difference to Average and Significance

Group	Value	Difference	SE	P-value	
2	0.938	-0.221	0.085	0.010	H
4	1.123	-0.036	0.116	0.755	
5	1.275	0.116	0.055	0.036	
6	1.239	0.080	0.058	0.167	

Note. The first thresholds is designated by $1.

parentheses in Table 3. The significance level used by Mplus at this stage is 0.001. As a result, some groups in the invariant set have p-values below 0.05 relative to the weighted average, but none have values below 0.001 (see rectangles labeled G and H in Table 5). Second, the pairwise contrasts are the starting point for the alignment method. Groups were initially "connected" if their pairwise contrast had a p-value larger than 0.01 (Asparouhov & Muthén, 2014, p. 5). In our example output, Groups 2 and 1 would have started as connected for the first threshold of BPI11 (p-value of 0.056) but not for BPI8 (p-value of 0.001) (see rectangles labeled B and A, respectively, in Table 5). The alignment method iterates from this starting point, calculating the weighted average for the connected groups, testing each group's estimated value against this weighted average, and excluding groups from the invariant set that has p-values below 0.001 relative to the weighted average. In short, it is expected that which groups are identified as invariant ("connected") and non-invariant differ between the first and final stage of the alignment method for multiple reasons, including the use of a p-value of 0.05 versus 0.001 as well as the use of pairwise contrasts versus contrasts to a weighted average.

Finally, we consider the R-square values. Recall that these R-square values indicate the degree to which variation of each loading and threshold parameter across groups in the configural model was explained by the alignment process. For instance, the value of 0.566 for Item 11's first threshold means that about 57 percent of the variation in these first threshold parameter estimates across groups in the configural model is explained by the alignment process. Since higher values indicate more invariance, in Table 5, we see that invariance is greater for this first threshold of Item 11 (0.566) than for Item 8 (0.280; compare rectangles I and J). Among the other items (not shown in Table 5), the first threshold has the greatest invariance for Items 12 (R-square = 0.960) and 16 (R-square = 0.984). That Items 12 and 16 have R-square values close to one is consistent with those items having no groups enclosed in parentheses for the first threshold in Table 3. In other words, the estimates of the first threshold are very similar across groups for Items 12 and 16, meaning these estimates are invariant. Said another way, there is evidence that group members are interpreting Items 12 and 16 similarly. The greatest non-invariance in the first threshold is evident for Item 14 (R-square = 0.089). That Item 14 has R-square value close to zero is consistent with Item 14 having two groups enclosed in parentheses for the first threshold in Table 3. In other words, the estimates of the first threshold are different for two of the groups relative to the rest of the groups for Item 14, and thus the estimates are non-invariant. Said another way, there is evidence that members of some groups are interpreting Item 14 differently than are members of other groups.

3.4 Running the `Harmony` R Package

A strength of the alignment method is that it can handle many groups, items, and categories. The amount of output quickly multiplies, however, as these numbers increase, making it difficult to draw meaning from the results. We created the `Harmony` R package to read the alignment output and report it in two ways. One report is a set of built-in graphs that allow for initial review of results. Another report is a set of csv-files that can be read into any software or spreadsheet package in order to create customized graphs, summary tables, and calculations. We illustrate key aspects of the `Harmony` output in the manuscript and offer a detailed step-by-step guide to `Harmony` in Online Appendix A.

3.4.1 Harmony Graphs of Thresholds and Loadings

The built-in graphs of thresholds produced by `Harmony` are shown in Figure 2. The *y*-axis lists the items within factors. The *x*-axis lists the threshold values. Groups are designated by colors, listed in the legend on the right (note that the `Harmony` package includes an option that allows users to choose different color scales, including those designed for persons who see colors differently, as illustrated in comparing Figures 2 and 3). Invariant and non-invariant values are distinguished by circles (invariant) and triangles (non-invariant). The weighted average for invariant groups is indicated by a black circle. The invariant and non-invariant groups and weighted average reflect the final stage of the iterative alignment algorithm. Note that the `Harmony` package orders the items in ascending order of the weighted average.

The graphs offer one strategy for concisely summarizing the results visually across many items and groups. The distinction between invariant and non-invariant groups is readily apparent by the triangles versus circles, with the magnitude of differences detectable visually in the distances between markers. As would be expected, for instance, the weighted average of invariant groups (black circles) falls within the invariant groups (colored circles), and the non-invariant groups (triangles) fall farther from them. The complementary value of the visual display relative to Mplus results is exemplified by comparing the results for the first thresholds of Items 8 and 11 – which we enclosed in rectangles in Figure 2 – to those we showed earlier. For Item 8 (rectangle labeled A in Figure 2), the blue and gold triangles represent Black females and Black males, respectively. These were the non-invariant groups for Item 8 discussed previously. Likewise, for Item 11 (rectangle labeled B in Figure 2), the orange and green triangles represent Latinos and White males, the groups discussed previously for Item 11. Figure 2 also depicts visually groups that were on the borderline

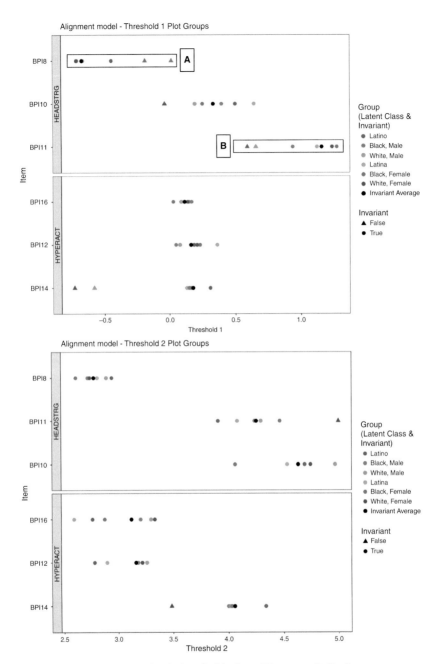

Figure 2 Graph of Thresholds from Harmony R-Package

Note. HEADSTRG = headstrong factor. HYPERACT = hyperactive factor. Groups are designated by colors, listed in the legend on the right. Invariant and non-invariant values are distinguished by circles (invariant) and triangles (non-invariant). The weighted average for invariant groups is indicated by a black circle. The invariant and non-invariant groups and weighted average reflect the final stage of the iterative alignment algorithm. Within each factor, the items are listed in ascending order based on these averages.

of invariant and non-invariant. For Item 8's first threshold (rectangle A), the orange circle representing Group 1 falls between the cluster of circles and the triangles. This result is consistent with the result in Table 5 that showed the *p*-value for Group 1's comparison with the weighted average of invariant groups was small (0.058) even though above the 0.001 threshold. Likewise, for Item 11, the gold circle representing Group 2 falls between the triangles and circles for the first threshold (rectangle B); this group had a *p*-value of 0.010 in Table 5 for the comparison with the invariant weighted average. In contrast, the blue circle representing Group 5 falls farthest in the other direction for Item 11's first threshold, and also had a small *p*-value in Table 5 (0.036).

Figure 3 shows similar graphs of the loadings. Here, the graph contains only circles and no triangles, consistent with none of the loadings being enclosed in

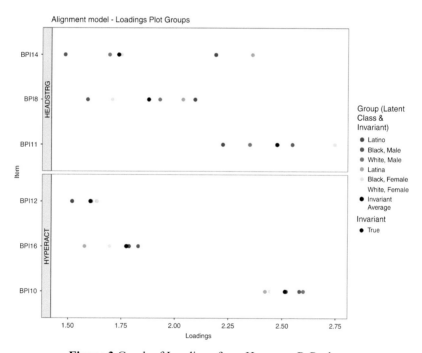

Figure 3 Graph of Loadings from Harmony R-Package

Note. HEADSTRG = headstrong factor. HYPERACT = hyperactive factor. Groups are designated by colors, listed in the legend on the right. Invariant and non-invariant values are distinguished by circles (invariant) and triangles (non-invariant). The weighted average for invariant groups is indicated by a black circle. Within each factor, the items are listed in ascending order based on these averages.

parentheses in Table 3. Visually, it appears the loadings have considerably more spread for Items 8 and 14 than the other items. Consistent with this spread, the R-square values are small for the loadings of Items 8 and 14 (at 0.000). Values were higher for Items 11 (0.112), 10 (0.686), 16 (0.895), and 12 (0.970). These results suggest that, in this case, the most extreme groups may differ from each other but not the weighted average. We return to this topic in the discussion, pointing to the need for more analytic and simulation studies of the alignment method (i.e., its algorithm focusing on identifying one set of invariant groups and one set of non-invariant groups may miss instances in which positive and negative deviations of the weighted average are offset).

3.4.2 Harmony Graphs of Cumulative Probability Curves and Category Probability Curves

Harmony also translates the parameter estimates from the IFA to IRT metric, converting loadings to discriminations and thresholds to difficulties, and uses these values to produce cumulative probability curves and category probability curves. Figure 4 shows Harmony's built-in graphs of these cumulative probability curves and category probability curves. Harmony allows the user to select which item and groups to graph. We chose Item 8 as an example, showing all six groups. We focus interpretation on Groups 3 (represented by the green curves) and Group 5 (represented by the blue curves). We listed the discriminations and difficulties for Groups 3 and 5 adjacent to the graphs. Recall that the discriminations determine the steepness of the curves. And, the difficulties determine the points at which the curves cross in the category probability curves and the points at which the curves reach 0.50 in the cumulative probability curves – see the vertical blue lines in the bottom graph.

Substantively, the category probability curves (top panel) tell us the probability (y-axis) that mothers of children from each group, including a White male (Group 3) and a Black female (Group 5), would report that it was *not true* (category 1), *sometimes true* (category 2), or *often true* (category 3) that her son or daughter "argues too much," at various levels of latent headstrongness (x-axis, θ_k).

Importantly, even given the same estimated latent level of the construct, we see that the probabilities of mothers' category choices differ between the groups. We used the straight blue lines to depict an example. The blue line intersects the x-axis at 0.4, representing a child with mid-range tendency toward headstrongness of latent level $\theta_k = 0.4$. The blue line intersects the blue curves (Group 5) at 0.55, as seen by the horizontal line extending to the y-axis. We

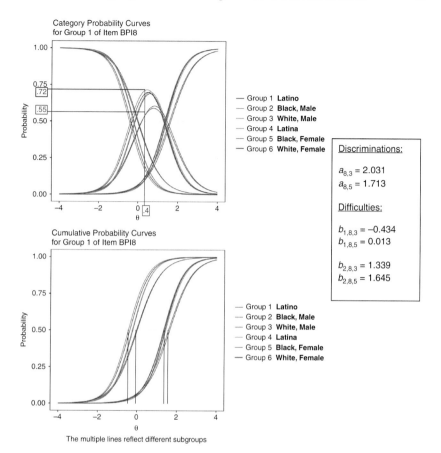

Figure 4 Graph of Category Probability Curves and Cumulative Probability
Curves from the Harmony R-Package

Note. The graphs are based on the IRT metric, which converted the loadings to discriminations and the thresholds to difficulties. Red vertical lines reflect the difficulty levels for each threshold (the point at which the cumulative probability curves reach 0.50).

interpret this result as demonstrating that the probability of the mother choosing *sometimes true* is 0.55 for Black females (Group 5) when their child has mid-range tendency toward headstrongness (latent level of $\theta_k = 0.4$). The blue line intersects the green curve (Group 3) at 0.72, again seen by the horizontal line extending to the *y*-axis. We interpret this result as demonstrating that the probability of the mother choosing *sometimes true* is 0.72 for White males (Group 3) when their child has mid-range tendency toward headstrongness (latent level of $\theta_k = 0.4$). Thus, for children with this same mid-range tendency toward headstrongness, mothers have a 0.17 (0.72–0.55) higher probability of choosing *sometimes true* for White males than for Black females on Item 8 (argues too much).

3.4.3 Harmony csv-Files and User Calculations

The Harmony R package places the item loadings and thresholds, and their standard errors, as well as the factor means and variances into csv-files. The values converted into the IRT-metric discriminations and difficulties are likewise saved along with the probabilities of the category and cumulative probability curves. With these results, analysts can create customized graphs and supplemental calculations.

3.5 Considering Substantive Size

3.5.1 Substantive Size of Parameter-Level Non-invariance

We used the `Harmony` csv-files of the discrimination and difficulty parameter estimates to calculate the Raju signed and unsigned areas. We again focus on the groups of White males (Group 3) and Black females (Group 5) and Item 8. Given the cumulative probability curves do not appear to cross between these two groups in Figure 4, it is as expected that the Raju signed and unsigned areas would be highly similar, in this case being 0.75 for both. In other words, holding latent tendency toward headstrongness constant, the tendency of mothers of White males to choose higher categories results in their children's expected score being 0.75 points higher than the expected score for Black females. In contrast, the signed and unsigned areas are smaller for Item 8 when comparing assigned sexes within race/ethnicity, being 0.10 for White males versus White females as well as for Black males versus Black females. This result is consistent with the similarity in the cumulative probability curves for these assigned sexes within race/ethnicities in Figure 4. Differences by sex within race/ethnicity are evident for other items, however. For instance, Item 11 (has strong temper and loses it easily), has areas of 0.69 for White males versus White females (signed and unsigned).

3.5.2 Substantive Size of Factor-Level Non-invariance

We provide two sets of graphs that capture the impact of adjusting for measurement non-invariance, in Figures 5 and 6. Both rely upon the averages of factor scores from the scalar model (which constrains all loadings and thresholds to be equal) and from the alignment method (which allows loadings and thresholds to vary, rotating their values to permit but minimize non-invariance). We standardized the factor scores (using the full-sample means and variances) before

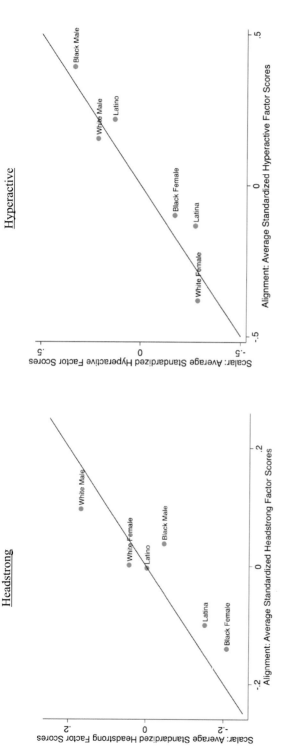

Figure 5 Graph of Average Factor Scores from Scalar and Alignment Method, in Standardized Metric

Note. Values are group-specific averages. Each set of factor scores (scalar, alignment) was standardized using the full sample mean and standard deviation. $n = 12,971$. Group sample sizes: Latino ($n = 1,112$), Black, male ($n = 2,158$), White, male ($n = 3,294$), Latina ($n = 977$), Black, female ($n = 2,149$), and, White, female ($n = 3,281$).

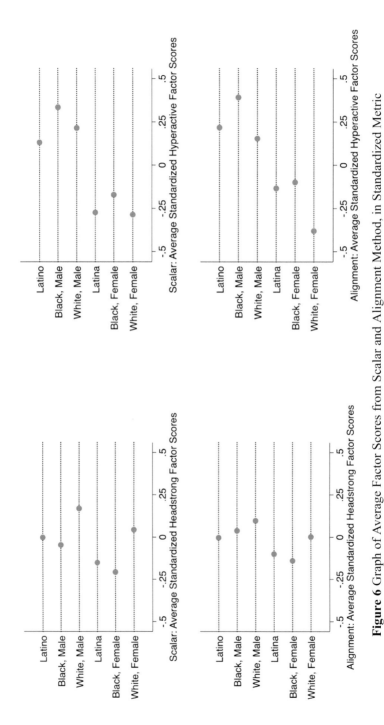

Figure 6 Graph of Average Factor Scores from Scalar and Alignment Method, in Standardized Metric

Note. $n = 12,971$. Group sample sizes: Latino ($n = 1,112$), Black, male ($n = 2,158$), White, male ($n = 3,294$), Latina ($n = 977$), Black, female ($n = 2,149$), and, White, female ($n = 3,281$). Each set of factor scores (scalar, alignment) is standardized using the full sample mean and standard deviation.

calculating the averages in order to facilitate comparison and to highlight the approximate substantive magnitude of differences. The first set of graphs plots the scalar scores against the aligned scores within each factor (headstrong and hyperactive). A line through the origin shows where the dots would fall if alignment had no impact at the factor score level (see Figure 5). The second set of graphs plots the average for each group within the scalar and alignment results. These results help visualize the ways in which the pattern of group means changes after alignment (see Figure 6). Online Appendix B shows the magnitude and significance of group mean differences.

Turning to interpretation, the scatterplots in Figure 5 show a similar pattern for both Headstrong and Hyperactive factors in the sense that the White male and White female groups are positioned above the 45-degree line, and the Black male, Black female, and Latina groups are positioned below the line. Specifically, in the left panel of Figure 5, the scatterplot of group means shows that the average aligned Headstrong factor scores were higher than the scalar averages for Black males (0.037 vs. −0.047, difference of 0.084), Latinas (−0.100 vs. −0.152, difference of 0.052), and Black females (−0.140 vs. −0.208, difference of 0.068). In contrast, the Headstrong averages for Latinos were nearly identical from the aligned and scalar models (−0.004 vs. −0.002, difference of −0.002). And, for White males and White females, Headstrong averages were lower from the aligned than scalar models (0.096 vs. 0.169, difference of −0.073; and 0.001 vs. 0.043, difference of −0.042, respectively). In the right panel of Figure 6, we again see the White males and females have lower aligned than scalar averages for the Hyperactive factor scores (0.154 vs. 0.215, difference of −0.061; and −0.381 vs. −0.286, difference of −0.095, respectively). Black males and females have somewhat higher aligned than scalar averages on these Hyperactive scores (0.392 vs. 0.334, difference of 0.058; and −0.099 vs. −0.171, difference of 0.072, respectively). The elevation of aligned versus scalar scores was even more pronounced for Latinos and females (0.218 vs. 0.131, difference of 0.087; and −0.134 vs. −0.274, difference of 0.140, respectively).

In Figure 6, we see the implications of these shifts in scores vis-à-vis group comparisons. Broadly, group differences are reduced for the Headstrong factor and accentuated for the Hyperactive factor with the aligned scores relative to the scalar scores. Specifically, whereas five pairs had Headstrong factor score averages that differed by at least |0.20| based on the scalar scores (Black females compared to Latinos, White males, and White females; Black males compared to White males; Latinas compared to White males), just one did based on the aligned scores (Black females relative to White males, with a magnitude reduced from |0.38| to |0.24|; see Online Appendix C). The relative positioning of Black males to Latinos also changed, although the two groups' averages did not differ significantly based on either the aligned or scalar factor scores. Regarding Hyperactive scores, the shift in relative position of White males' and White females' scores was especially salient, each positioned farther to the left (lower) than the other two racial-ethnic groups identified as the same assigned sex. White females had an average score >0.20 in magnitude smaller than Latinas (-0.25, $p < 0.05$) and Black females (-0.28, $p < 0.05$) for the aligned scores but not for the scalar scores (-0.01, $p > 0.05$ and -0.12, $p < 0.05$, respectively). A similar change was evident for White males versus Black males, with a difference of -0.24 ($p < 0.05$) based on the aligned scores versus -0.12 ($p < 0.05$) for the scalar scores.

3.5.3 Potential Interpretations and Limitations of Empirical Example

We offer some potential interpretations of the results of our empirical example in order to encourage their replication and extension, and to encourage the application of the alignment method to examine substantive questions for other measures and samples. As we do so, we note that our example was limited in ways that should be kept in mind when interpreting and generalizing the results. In other words, we featured just six of the thirty-two BPI items, just six intersectional groups defined by the child's assigned binary sex (male/female) and three race/ethnicities (Black, Latina/o, White), and relied upon two datasets (C-NLSY79, PSID-CDS) from which we chose one wave for each child across three decades. Replication and extension with additional items from the BPI and other measures of children's behaviors (including those created in collaboration with members of each group), additional sex/gender and racial/ethnic identities (including children's self-identifications), and other samples (including considering variation across regions/locales, historical time, and additional characteristics of children, parents, and their families). In short, we encourage future studies that place the alignment method in the context of the broader approaches we discussed involving multi-stakeholder, multi-method iterative interrogations of the measure informed by theory and practice and inclusive of the groups being studied.

At the same time that our example results are tentative, this empirical illustration suggests that replication and extension should be prioritized, given our results demonstrate the importance of considering that mothers of children assigned as boys or girls and as Black, Latina/o, and White may perceive and report about their behaviors differently. The potential for differences in reference points and social desirability are well known (Duckworth & Yeager, 2015), yet their examination is more common in the methodological than substantive journals (Gordon, 2015). In relation to the BPI, this tutorial demonstrates how using the alignment method can advance upon historical studies that have used less robust strategies for considering potential non-invariance and have relied upon raw or normed scores for group comparisons. For instance, one study subtracted base year within racial-ethnic group averages from individual scores (McLoyd & Smith, 2002), another used predicted BPI scores adjusted for race, sex, and age (Cleveland et al., 2000), and another simply noted the limitation of potential different meaning of the items by age (Jackson & Mare, 2007). Some published studies have identified non-invariance for some BPI items by race-ethnicity at particular waves in the CNLSY-79 (Guttmannova et al., 2008; McLeod et al., 1994; Spencer et al., 2005), and differential item functioning has been identified with IRT models applied to the BPI in other samples (Studts et al., 2017). Yet, the alignment method and associated `Harmony` R package will make it easier for substantive scholars to pursue more comprehensive studies of invariance by multiple demographic characteristics with the CNLSY-79 and PSID-CDS.

In the empirical example, item-level non-invariance was primarily evident at the threshold level. Adjusting for such differences was consequential for the mean scale score differences among groups. For instance, an item asking mothers to rate whether their child "argues too much" demonstrated significant and meaningful differences at the threshold level between White males and Black females. When the model equated children in terms of their latent "headstrongness," mothers of White males were more likely to say that it was "sometimes true" that their child "argues too much" than were mothers of Black females. These item-level differences were meaningfully sized, such as a seventeen percentage point difference in choosing the category at one latent level. The kinds of future studies just called for might interrogate this finding, seeing if it replicates empirically with applications of the alignment method to other samples and inviting mothers and other stakeholders representing the studied groups to offer their interpretive insights through in-depth and cognitive interviews and focus groups. Rious et al. (2019), for instance, called for rethinking what had been labeled "hostile" African American parenting styles given Eurocentric norms were inadequate for capturing approaches that facilitated youth development by anticipating conflict in the context of high warmth and cultural socialization. At the group-mean level of the latent "headstrongness" construct, we found that adjusting for this item-level non-invariance – and non-invariance evident for other "headstrong" items and groups – reduced the magnitude of the mean difference between White males and Black females in estimated "headstrongness" by 0.14 standard deviations. Again, future interrogation of this finding would be informative. Engaging a diverse group of stakeholders to support their understanding of how the alignment method makes such an adjustment (and the ways other strategies for measurement invariance and differential item functioning do so) can enrich dialogue about when and where their use improves fairness and equity in reports of measures' summary scores, and when and where it does not. Such stakeholders can enter long-standing debates, for instance, about the extent to which item-level invariance is noteworthy, even when group-level averages are equivalent. In other words, is it equally important to recognize how different people interpret items, as to adjust for such differences in order to focus on group mean differences in measure-level scores?

4 Discussion

This tutorial demonstrated how to use the alignment method to achieve the important goal of ensuring that the measurement invariance aspect of measurement fairness is achieved and, where it is not, to elevate the visibility of measurement non-invariance. Explaining the concepts and formulas underlying the method as well as demonstrating how to apply it in Mplus and how to read, summarize, and interpret the results supports more psychologists using the method. By focusing on the application of the alignment method to multi-category items, we support such use with common item types in the field. When scholars instead treat categorical items as continuous, a single intercept per item is estimated, and non-invariance at specific boundaries of certain categories may be overlooked. Testing for such differences in boundary thresholds is needed in order to fully interrogate how groups differ in interpreting items and in order to ensure comparisons of group means on the latent construct are fair (i.e., that their "zero points" are the same). Differences across groups in factor loadings are also identified by the alignment method applied to categorical items, with implications for the scale of the items. Identifying loading differences, and adjusting for them, is essential to ensuring that the unit (i.e., what "one more" means) is the same across groups. This result has implications for the strength of associations of scale scores with predictors and outcomes across groups (i.e., tests of interactions in regression models).

4.1 What the Alignment Method Offers to Developmental Scientists

This tutorial has demonstrated the great potential of the alignment method for developmental scientists, including achieving measurement fairness across many groups, treating items as categorical, and allowing for partial non-invariance.

4.1.1 Achieving Measurement Fairness across Many Groups (Including Intersectionality)

Developmental science has begun to recognize the hegemonic origins of many of its theories and methods, representing dominant groups within nations as well as in Global West and North paradigms and rarely reflecting diversity across genders, race/ethnicities, socio-economic backgrounds, and other characteristics. The field has an opportunity to accelerate progress in being more equitable, inclusive, and just, by representing the peoples and paradigms that are indigenous to studied contexts, including those from marginalized communities within nations and in the Global East and South (Lee & Wong, 2022; Shute & Slee, 2015). The alignment method is one approach for empirically supporting such progress, being particularly well suited for considering multilayered identities. Designed to accommodate many groups, the alignment method facilitates examination of the intersection of numerous identities, going beyond the single variables (e.g., assigned sex, assigned race/ethnicity) examined individually typical of prior measurement invariance studies. The alignment method complements other recent extensions of the MIMIC model to interactions among multiple covariates. Under certain specifications, equivalent results would be obtained when multilayered groups are defined versus their underlying variables being interacted. Yet, the alignment method facilitates making visible multilayered groups sharing multiple identities, foregrounding their collective identities as in person-centered approaches. Presentation of each multilayered group also makes clear variation in sample size across groups, and thus the degree to which their parameters can be precisely estimated. Such results point to the need to qualify current results, where statistical power is limited, and to improve future designs to better represent groups with equitable statistical power. A strength of the alignment method is to make it straightforward to identify both the groups' own parameter estimates and which groups' estimates are statistically equivalent.

4.1.2 Appropriately Treating Items as Categorical (Identifying Threshold Non-invariance)

Tutorials and applications of the alignment approach to date have focused on models for continuous items. Yet, many psychological studies rely upon measures that have multi-category questions. The extensions of the alignment approach to multi-category questions are straightforward from a statistical standpoint, relying upon well-established psychometric models for multi-category items. Yet, as with other statistical advances, widespread implementation including by substantive scholars and applied researchers requires support including making it easy to understand, implement, and interpret the results. This tutorial explained and exemplified interpretation of the parameters estimated by the alignment method applied to multi-category items, including walking through where to locate and understand values in the Mplus output. We also demonstrated how our openly available `Harmony` R package makes it easy to calculate and graph results in the predicted probability units that can support a wide array of stakeholders drawing meaning from the results. Importantly, we also explained why and showed how it is invariance at the level of item thresholds that impacts group mean differences in measure scores. In contrast, invariance at the level of item loadings impacts group variances in measure scores. When the focus of a study is group mean differences, it is thus essential for developmental scholars to go beyond examination of testing for invariance in factor loadings and to also test for invariance in factor thresholds.

4.1.3 Allowing for Partial Non-Invariance (Without Requiring "Manual" Iterative Processes)

Historical applications of multi-group factor analysis sometimes focused on model-level testing of the relative fit of configural, metric, and scalar models. These models focus on full invariance and full non-invariance, by freely estimating all loadings and thresholds across groups versus fixing as equal the loadings and/or thresholds. These all or nothing models can overlook situations of partial invariance, wherein some groups have statistically equivalent load-ings or thresholds and others differ. Partial invariance can be informative substantively, allowing scholars and other stakeholders to test theories and expectations about which groups' responses to certain items would be more similar and which more different. Partial invariance also allows for the devel-opment and use of measures that allow for such similarities and differences; when most item loadings and thresholds operate similarly across groups, meas-ure-level scores can be estimated while allowing for some differences in item loadings and thresholds. The alignment method makes it easier for substantive scholars to identify and adjust for partial invariance. As discussed earlier, we encourage collaborative efforts to interpret and report about item-level differ-ences as these adjusted measure scores are interpreted and reported.

4.2 What the Alignment Method Doesn't (Yet) Do

4.2.1 Need for More Theoretical and Simulation Studies

We encourage continued research and extension of the alignment model itself. Our empirical example suggested, for instance, that the alignment method might miss instances in which the most extreme groups may differ from each other but not the weighted average of the invariant groups. We therefore encourage future analytic and simulation studies of whether adjustments to the algorithm may be needed to detect such differences. For example, currently, the algorithm focuses on identifying one set of invariant groups. This approach may overlook instances in which there is more than one invariant set – for example, there might be two invariant sets whose groups are similar within each set but different between the two sets. The focus on a single invariant set may also overlook instances in which all groups vary considerably from one another, but no set exists whose groups are consistently similar to each other – for example, as in the patterns evident for the loadings of our empirical example.

Related to these considerations of numbers and types of invariant groups, the alignment method as implemented in Mplus relies upon specific cutoffs for p-values (0.01 to determine initially connected groups; 0.001 to later add groups to an invariant set). In early presentation of the alignment method, Asparouhov and Muthén (2014, p. 5) stated that "The algorithm is based on multiple pairwise comparisons; that is, multiple testing is done and to avoid false non-invariance discovery, we use smaller p-values than the nominal 0.05." Future simulation and empirical work might examine robustness of results under varying criteria and support users having flexibility to use other criteria, including depending on numbers of groups and on sample sizes as in family-wide criteria for hypothesis testing.

Also of value would be expansion of simulations testing regarding how the alignment method compares to other approaches (DeMars, 2020; Finch, 2016; Kim et al., 2017; Wen & Hu, 2022), including to further consider the circumstances under which the alignment method picks up equally well nonuniform and uniform DIF (i.e., differential item functioning). We also encourage continued research on strategies similar to the alignment method and extensions of the alignment method. Examples include applications of machine learning techniques (Belzak & Bauer, 2020) and the Gini Index (Strobl et al., 2021) in DIF contexts, a deep neural network approach to measurement invariance (Pokropek & Pokropek, 2022), use of alignment in growth modeling (Lai, 2021), and demonstration of how to use the alignment results as start values for a confirmatory factor analytic model that might be embedded within a broader structural equation model (Marsh et al., 2018). The rough rule of thumb of a limit of 25 percent non-invariance for trustworthy alignment results (Muthén & Asparouhov, 2014, p. 3) would also benefit from additional simulation research. Likewise, potential criteria for the R-square measure might be examined in future simulation studies, including the degree to which interpretations of R-square may be application-specific. In other words, similar to distinguishing between explainable (systematic error) and unexplainable ("pure" error) for R-square values in OLS, it may be that interpretation of R-square in the alignment context depends on factors such as the extent of parameter variation across groups. Also warranting further attention is consideration of various fit indices and information criteria to identify well-fitting models and choose among them, recognizing that "the quest for standard cutoff criterion for each of the fit indices has proven to be elusive . . . [and as] fit indices are applied beyond CFA models to more complex models – multiple group models, multilevel models, growth models, and so forth – this quest for a single, standard cutoff criterion becomes increasingly chimerical and alternative strategies are needed" (West et al., 2012, pp. 227–228).

More attention and guidance are also needed for total sample size, sample size within each group, and number of cases within each response category. The limited simulation research with the alignment method found results are less trustworthy when non-invariance exceeds the 25 percent criterion if sample sizes were smaller, meaning 100 versus 1,000 cases in the simulation (Muthén & Asparouhov, 2014, p. 3). Other research on measurement invariance has recommended 500 study participants in each focal subgroup (Tay et al., 2014). A power simulation demonstrated uniformly high power for $n = 400$ when testing invariance in factor loadings for continuous items (Meade & Bauer, 2007) and recent simulations verified adequate power with the standard sample sizes of several hundred for test linking based on dichotomous items (Babcock & Hodge, 2020). As future research considers these topics, the incorporation of additional IRT models into the alignment approach and consideration of sensitivity of results to them offers an additional important line of inquiry. IRT models that estimate more parameters require larger sample sizes, yet can be of value such as when testing assumptions of ordinality (Fujimoto et al., 2018).

We also featured an example in which all items had the same response structure, although the graded response model can accommodate items with different numbers of response categories. The `Harmony` R package can read results with items having such differing response structures. The `Harmony` package also flags empirical variation in a number of categories, when items have the same response structure but some items have no cases in a particular category for one or more groups. Scrutinizing such items is important, as Mplus provides results in such situations, but the meaning of estimated thresholds would vary across groups. Users can also use the `Harmony` package to screen for small cell sizes. As is the case for total and group sample sizes, however, no single-decision rule exists to determine how small is too small and what to do. For instance, one rule of thumb recommends scrutiny of categories with fewer than ten cases. When a dataset has categories below this threshold, some analysts might conclude that the sample size is insufficient or that the instrument is not well suited for the sample. Other analysts might consider collapsing adjacent categories or excluding certain items. Others might turn to combining multiple datasets (Fujimoto et al., 2018). The extent to which differences in cell sizes across groups affect the detection of invariance by the alignment method is another important area of future research (Yoon & Lai, 2018). Across all of these efforts, more guidance for users regarding sample sizes for desired precision of estimation and statistical power is needed, including for total sample size, sample size within each group, and number of cases within each response category.

4.2.2 Potential for Bayesian Approaches

The alignment method developers introduced a Bayesian estimation approach to measurement invariance (Muthén & Asparouhov, 2013) as an extension to their previous work on Bayesian structural equation modeling (Muthén & Asparouhov, 2012). Although just a few studies seem to have used or studied Bayesian measurement invariance (e.g., De Bondt & Van Petegem, 2015; Lai et al., 2022; Muthén & Asparouhov, 2018; Pokropek et al., 2020; Winter & Depaoli, 2020), there are at least four good reasons to further explore the use of Bayesian estimation for measurement invariance. First, the numerical integration in maximum likelihood estimation becomes computationally intractable in presence of high-dimensional instruments. Thus, the study of measurement invariance for multidimensional instruments would benefit from Bayesian approaches. Second, exact zero differences in factor loadings and thresholds can be replaced with approximate zeros. From a theoretical perspective, exact zero would only make sense when groups are exact replications of each other. Otherwise, it should be expected that there are at least some small differences in the loadings and thresholds estimations across groups. Third, current implementation of measurement alignment relies on p-values (with $p > 0.01$ used to connect groups at the initial stage, and $p > 0.001$ to add groups to the invariant set at the later stages). Although frequentist hypothesis testing can (and should) be corrected for family-wise error, the interpretation under Bayesian inference avoids the dichotomy presented by the frequentist hypothesis testing when interpreting results. Fourth, the current implementation in Mplus allows for specifying the estimation as Bayesian in the analysis. However, the user has limited flexibility in the choices of priors; expanding the choices and considering the impacts of additional priors would be desirable.

4.3 Concluding Remarks

In sum, the alignment method is a promising strategy to support psychologists ensuring that measures achieve the invariance aspect of fairness across groups. By making it easier to test for differences in item functioning across many groups, psychologists can begin to consider the intersection of demographic and other characteristics as we did by looking at assigned sex and race/ethnicity together in our empirical example. The Harmony R package we provide also simplifies the process of reading and visualizing results in ways that allow substantive scholars to draw meaning from them. As such, this tutorial helps researchers elevate theorizing and testing for measurement invariance across groups at the item level to be on par with theorizing and testing about group mean differences (Gordon, 2015). When they substantively and empirically scrutinize measurement invariance, scholars either ensure that the "ruler" measuring constructs is consistent across social groups or recognize that rulers vary across groups (and possibly some groups eschew rulers), thereby improving the accuracy and fairness of substantive conclusions about levels and correlates of these constructs across groups.

References

Achenbach System of Empirically Based Assessment (ASEBA). (n.d.). *The ASEBA approach*. https://aseba.org/.

Aiken, L. S., West, S. G., & Millsap, R. E. (2008). Doctoral training in statistics, measurement, and methodology in psychology: Replication and extension. *American Psychologist*, *63*, 32–50. https://doi.org/10.1037/0003-066X.63.1.32.

American Educational Research Association (AERA), American Psychological Association (APA), & National Council on Measurement in Education (NCME). (2014). *Standards for educational and psychological testing*. American Educational Research Association. www.testingstandards.net/open-access-files.html.

Asparouhov, T., & Muthén, B. (2014). Multiple-group factor analysis alignment. *Structural Equation Modeling: A Multidisciplinary Journal*, *21*(4), 495–508. https://doi.org/10.1080/10705511.2014.919210.

Asparouhov, T., & Muthén, B. (2020, December). *IRT in Mplus* (Version 4). www.statmodel.com/download/MplusIRT.pdf.

Asparouhov, T., & Muthén, B. (2023). Multiple group alignment for exploratory and structural equation models. *Structural Equation Modeling.*, *30*(2), 169–191 https://doi.org/10.1080/10705511.2022.2127100.

Babcock, B., & Hodge, K. J. (2020). Rasch versus classical equating in the context of small sample sizes. *Educational and Psychological Measurement*, *80*, 499–521. https://doi.org/10.1177/0013164419878483.

Bansal, P. S., Babinski, D. E., Waxmonsky, J. G., & Waschbusch, D. A. (2022). Psychometric properties of parent ratings on the Inventory of Callous–Unemotional Traits in a nationally representative sample of 5- to 12-year-olds. *Assessment*, *29*, 242–256. https://doi.org/10.1177/1073191120964562.

Bauer, D. J. (2017). A more general model for testing measurement invariance and differential item functioning. *Psychological Methods*, *22*, 507–526. https://doi.org/10.1037/met0000077.

Belzak, W. C. M., & Bauer, D. J. (2020). Improving the assessment of measurement invariance: Using regularization to select anchor items and identify differential item functioning. *Psychological Methods*, *25*, 673–690. https://doi.org/10.1037/met0000253.

Benjamin, L. T., Jr. (2005). A history of clinical psychology as a profession in America (and a glimpse at its future). *Annual Review of Clinical Psychology*, *1*, 1–30. https://doi.org/10.1146/annurev.clinpsy.1.102803.143758.

Bodenhorn, T., Burns, J. P., & Palmer, M. (2020). Change, contradiction, and the state: Higher education in greater China. *The China Quarterly*, *244*, 903–919. https://doi.org/10.1017/S0305741020001228.

Bordovsky, J. T., Krueger, R. F., Argawal, A., & Grucza, R. A. (2019). A decline in propensity toward risk behaviors among U. S. adolescents. *Journal of Adolescent Health*, *65*, 745–751. https://doi.org/10.1016/j.jadohealth.2019.07.001.

Boulkedid, R., Abdoul, H., Loustau, M., Sibony, O., & Alberti, C. (2011). Using and reporting the Delphi method for selecting healthcare quality indicators: A systematic review. *PloS One*, *6*(6), e20476. https://doi.org/10.1371/journal.pone.0020476.

Bratt, C., Abrams, D., Swift, H. J., Vauclair, C. M., & Marques, S. (2018). Perceived age discrimination across age in Europe: From an ageing society to a society for all ages. *Developmental Psychology*, *54*, 167–180. https://doi.org/10.1037/dev0000398.

Burnham, K. P., & Anderson, D. R. (2002). *Model selection and multi-model inference*. Springer-Verlag.

Buss, A. H., & Perry, M. P. (1992). The aggression questionnaire. *Journal of Personality and Social Psychology*, *63*, 452–459. https://doi.org/10.1037/0022-3514.63.3.452.

Buss, A. H., & Warren, W. L. (2000). *Aggression questionnaire*. WPS. www.wpspublish.com/aq-aggression-questionnaire.

Byrne, B. M., Oakland, T., Leong, F. T. L. et al. (2009). A critical analysis of cross-cultural research and testing practices: Implications for improved education and training in psychology. *Training and Education in Professional Psychology*, *3*, 94–105. https://doi.org/10.1037/a0014516.

Byrne, B. M., Shavelson, R. J., & Muthén, B. (1989). Testing for the equivalence of factor covariance and mean structures: The issue of partial measurement invariance. *Psychological Bulletin*, *105*(3), 456–466. https://doi.org/10.1037/0033-2909.105.3.456.

Camilli, G. (2006). Test fairness. In R. L. Brennan (Ed.), *Educational measurement* (4th ed., pp. 221–256). Praeger.

Cheung, G. W., & Lau, R. S. (2012). A direct comparison approach for testing measurement invariance. *Organizational Research Methods*, *15*, 167–198. https://doi.org/10.1177/1094428111421987.

Chilisa, B. (2020). *Indigenous research methodologies*. Sage.

Cleveland, H. H., Wiebe, R. P., van den Oord, E. J. C. G., & Rowe, D. C. (2000). Behavior problems among children from different family structures: The influence of genetic self-selection. *Child Development*, *71*, 733–751. https://doi.org/10.1111/1467-8624.00182.

Covarrubias, A., & Vélez, V. (2013). Critical race quantitative intersectionality: An antiracist research paradigm that refuses to "let the numbers speak for themselves." In M. Lynn & A. D. Dixson (Eds.), *Handbook of critical race theory in education* (pp. 270–285). Routledge.

Crenshaw, K. (1989). Demarginalizing the intersection of race and sex: A black feminist critique of antidiscrimination doctrine, feminist theory and antiracist politics. *University of Chicago Legal Forum, 1989 (1)*, Article 8, 139–167.

Crowder, M. K., Gordon, R. A., Brown, R. D., Davidson, L. A., & Domitrovich, C. E. (2019). Linking social and emotional learning standards to the WCSD Social-Emotional Competency Assessment: A Rasch approach. *School Psychology Quarterly, 34*, 281–295. https://doi.org/10.1037/spq0000308.

Davidov, E., Meuleman, B., Cieciuch, J., Schmidt, P., & Billiet, J. (2014). Measurement equivalence in cross-national research. *Annual Review of Sociology, 40*, 55–75. https://doi.org/10.1146/annurev-soc-071913-043137.

De Bondt, N., & Van Petegem, P. (2015). Psychometric evaluation of the overexcitability questionnaire-two applying Bayesian structural equation modeling (BSEM) and multiple-group BSEM-based alignment with approximate measurement invariance. *Frontiers in Psychology*, 6, 1963. https://doi.org/10.3389/fpsyg.2015.01963.

DeMars, C. E. (2020). Alignment as an alternative to anchor purification in DIF analyses. *Structural Equation Modeling, 27*, 56–72. https://doi.org/10.1080/10705511.2019.1617151.

Dorans, N. J., & Cook, L. L. (2016). *Fairness in educational assessment and measurement*. Routledge. https://doi.org/10.4324/9781315774527.

Duckworth, A. L., & Yeager, D. S. (2015). Measurement matters: Assessing personal qualities other than cognitive ability for educational purposes. *Educational Researcher, 44*, 237–251. https://doi.org/10.3102/0013189X15584327.

Embretson, S. E., & Reise, S. P. (2000). *Item response theory for psychologists*. Lawrence Erlbaum Associates.

Evers, A., Muñiz, J., Hagemeister, C. et al. (2013). Assessing the quality of tests: Revision of the European Federation of Psychologists' Associations (EFPA) review model. *Psichothema, 25*, 283–291.

Finch, W. H. (2016). Detection of differential item functioning for more than two groups: A Monte Carlo comparison of methods. *Applied Measurement in Education, 29*, 30–45. https://doi.org/10.1080/08957347.2015.1102916.

Flake, J. K., Pek, J., & Hehman, E. (2017). Construct validation in social and personality research: Current practice and recommendations. *Social Psychological and Personality Science, 8*, 370–378. https://doi.org/10.1177/1948550617693063.

Fujimoto, K. A., Gordon, R. A., Peng, F., & Hofer, K. G. (2018). Examining the category functioning of the ECERS-R across eight datasets. *AERA Open*, *4*, 1–16. https://doi.org/10.1177/2332858418758299.

Garcia, N. M., López, N., & Vélez, V. N. (2018). QuantCrit: Rectifying quantitative methods through critical race theory. *Race Ethnicity and Education*, *21*, 149–157. https://doi.org/10.1080/13613324.2017.1377675.

Golinski, C., & Cribbie, R. A. (2009). The expanding role of quantitative methodologists in advancing psychology. *Canadian Psychology*, *50*, 83–90. https://doi.org/10.1037/a0015180.

Gordon, R. A. (2015). Measuring constructs in family science: How can IRT improve precision and validity? *Journal of Marriage and Family*, *77*, 147–176. https://doi.org/10.1111/jomf.12157.

Gordon, R. A., Crowder, M. K., Aloe, A. M., Davidson, L. A., & Domitrovich, C. E. (2022). Student self-ratings of social-emotional competencies: Dimensional structure and outcome associations of the WCSD-SECA among Hispanic and non-Hispanic White boys and girls in elementary through high school. *Journal of School Psychology*, *93*, 41–62. https://doi.org/10.1016/j.jsp.2022.05.002.

Gordon, R. A., & Davidson, L. A. (2022). Cross-cutting issues for measuring SECs in context: General opportunities and challenges with an illustration of the Washoe County School District Social-Emotional Competency Assessment (WCSD-SECAs). In S. Jones, N. Lesaux, & S. Barnes (Eds.), *Measuring non-cognitive skills in school settings* (pp. 225–251). Guilford Press.

Guttmannova, K., Szanyi, J. M., & Cali, P. W. (2008). Internalizing and externalizing behavior problem scores: Cross-ethnic and longitudinal measurement invariance of the Behavior Problem Index. *Educational and Psychological Measurement*, *68*, 676–694. https://doi.org/10.1177/0013164407310127.

Han, K., Colarelli, S. M., & Weed, N. C. (2019). Methodological and statistical advances in the consideration of cultural diversity in assessment: A critical review of group classification and measurement invariance testing. *Psychological Assessment*, *31*, 1481–1496. https://doi.org/10.1037/pas0000731.

Hauser, R. M., & Goldberger, A. S. (1971). The treatment of unobservable variables in path analysis. *Sociological Methodology*, *3*, 81–117. https://doi.org/10.2307/270819.

Hui, C. H., & Triandis, H. C. (1985). Measurement in cross-cultural psychology: A review and comparison of strategies. *Journal of Cross-Cultural Psychology*, *16*, 131–152. https://doi.org/10.1177/0022002185016002001.

Hussey, I., & Hughes, S. (2020). Hidden invalidity among 15 commonly used measures in social and personality psychology. *Advances in Methods and Practices in Psychological Science, 3*, 166–184. https://doi.org/10.1177/251524 5919882903.

Jackson, M. I., & Mare, R. D. (2007). Cross-sectional and longitudinal measurements of neighborhood experience and their effects on children. *Social Science Research, 36*, 590–610. https://doi.org/10.1016/j.ssresearch.2007.02.002.

Johnson, J. L., & Geisinger, K. F. (2022). *Fairness in educational and psychological testing: Examining theoretical, research, practice, and policy implications of the 2014 standards.* American Educational Research Association. https://doi.org/10.3102/9780935302967_1.

Kim, E. S., Cao, C., Wang, Y., & Nguyen, D. T. (2017). Measurement invariance testing with many groups: A comparison of five approaches. *Structural Equation Modeling, 24*, 524–544. https://doi.org/10.1080/10705511.2017.1304822.

King, K. M., Pullman, M. D., Lyon, A. R., Dorsey, S., & Lewis, C. C. (2019). Using implementation science to close the gap between the optimal and typical practice of quantitative methods in clinical science. *Journal of Abnormal Psychology, 128*, 547–562. https://doi.org/10.1037/abn0000417.

Kolen, M. J., & Brennan, R. L. (2014). *Test equating, scaling, and linking.* Springer. https://doi.org/10.1007/978-1-4939-0317-7.

Lai, M. H. C. (2021). Adjusting for measurement noninvariance with alignment in growth modeling. *Multivariate Behavioral Research.* https://doi.org/10.1080/00273171.2021.1941730.

Lai, M. H. C., Liu, Y., & Tse, W. W. (2022). Adjusting for partial invariance in latent parameter estimation: Comparing forward specification search and approximate invariance methods. *Behavior Research Methods, 54*, 414–434. https://doi.org/10.3758/s13428-021-01560-2.

Lane, S., Raymond, M. R., & Haladyna, T. M. (2016). *Handbook of test development.* Routledge.

Lansford, J. E., Rothenberg, W. A., Riley, J. et al. (2021). Longitudinal trajectories of four domains of parenting in relation to adolescent age and puberty in nine countries. *Child Development, 92*, e493–e512. https://doi.org/10.1111/cdev.13526.

Lee, J., & Wong, K. K. (2022). *Centering whole-child development in global education reform international perspectives on agendas for educational equity and quality.* Routledge. https://doi.org/10.4324/9781003202714.

Lemann, N. (2000). *The big test: The secret history of American meritocracy.* Farrar, Straus, and Giroux.

Likert, R. (1932). A technique for the measurement of attitudes. *Archives of Psychology, 22*(140), 1–55.

Liu, Y., Millsap, R. E., West, S. G. et al. (2017). Testing measurement invariance in longitudinal data with ordered-categorical measures. *Psychological Methods*, *22*, 486–506. https://doi.org/10.1037/met0000075.

Long, J. S. (1997). *Regression models for categorical and limited dependent variables*. Sage.

Long, J. S., & Freese, J. (2014). *Regression models for categorical dependent variables using Stata* (3rd ed.). Stata Press.

Luong, R., & Flake, J. K. (2022). Measurement invariance testing using confirmatory factor analysis and alignment optimization: A tutorial for transparent analysis planning and reporting. *Psychological Methods*. https://doi.org/10.1037/met0000441.

Marsh, H. W., Guo, J., Parker, P. D. et al. (2018). What to do when scalar invariance fails: The extended alignment method for multi-group factor analysis comparison of latent means across many groups. *Psychological Methods*, *23*, 524–545. https://doi.org/10.1037/met0000113.

McLeod, J. D., Kruttschnitt, C., & Dornfeld, M. (1994). Does parenting explain the effects of structural conditions on children's antisocial behavior? A comparison of Blacks and Whites. *Social Forces*, *73*, 575–604. https://doi.org/10.2307/2579822.

McLoyd, V., & Smith, J. (2002). Physical discipline and behavior problems in African American, European American, and Hispanic children: Emotional support as a moderator. *Journal of Marriage and Family*, *64*, 40–53. https://doi.org/10.1111/j.1741-3737.2002.00040.x.

Meade, A. W. (2010). A taxonomy of effect size measures for the differential functioning of items and scales. *The Journal of Applied Psychology*, *95*(4), 728–743. https://doi.org/10.1037/a0018966.

Meade, A. W., & Bauer, D. J. (2007). Power and precision in confirmatory factor analytic tests of measurement invariance. *Structural Equation Modeling*, *14*, 611–635. https://doi.org/10.1080/10705510701575461.

Meitinger, K., Davidov, E., Schmidt, P., & Braun, M. (2020). Measurement invariance: Testing for it and explaining why it is absent. *Survey Research Methods*, *14*, 345–349.

Messick, S. (1989). Meaning and values in test validation: The science and ethics of assessment. *Educational Researcher*, *18*, 5–11. https://doi.org/10.3102/0013189X018002005.

Millsap, R. E. (2011). *Statistical approaches to measurement invariance*. Routledge. https://doi.org/10.4324/9780203821961.

Morrell, L., Collier, T., Black, P., & Wilson, M. (2017). A construct-modeling approach to develop a learning progression of how students understand the structure of matter. *Journal of Research in Science Teaching, 54*, 1024–1048. https://doi.org/10.1002/tea.21397.

Moss, P. A. (2016). Shifting the focus of validity for test use. *Assessment in Education, 23*, 1–16. https://doi.org/10.1080/0969594X.2015.1072085.

Moss, P. A., Pullin, D., Gee, J. P., & Haertel, E. H. (2005). The idea of testing: Psychometric and sociocultural perspectives. *Measurement, 3*, 63–83. https://doi.org/10.1207/s15366359mea0302_1.

Muthén, B., & Asparouhov, T. (2012). Bayesian structural equation modeling: A more flexible representation of substantive theory. *Psychological Methods, 17*, 313–335. https://doi.org/10.1037/a0026802.

Muthén, B., & Asparouhov, T. (2013). *BSEM measurement invariance analysis.* Mplus Web Notes: No. 17. www.statmodel.com.

Muthén, B., & Asparouhov, T. (2014). IRT studies of many groups: The alignment method. *Frontiers in Psychology, 5*. https://doi.org/10.3389/fpsyg.2014.00978.

Muthén, B., & Asparouhov, T. (2018). Recent methods for the study of measurement invariance with many groups: Alignment and random effects. *Sociological Methods & Research, 47*(4), 637–664. https://doi.org/10.1177/0049124117701488.

Nering, M., & Ostini, R. (Eds.). (2010). *Handbook of polytomous item response theory models.* Routledge. https://doi.org/10.4324/9780203861264.

Oakland, T., Douglas, S., & Kane, H. (2016). Top ten standardized tests used internationally with children and youth by school psychologists in 64 countries: A 24-year follow-up study. *Journal of Psychoeducational Assessment, 34*, 166–176. https://doi.org/10.1177/0734282915595303.

Osterlind, S. J., & Everson, H. T. (2009). *Differential item functioning* (2nd ed.). Sage. https://doi.org/10.4135/9781412993913.

Parcel, T. L., & Menaghan, E. G. (1988). *Measuring behavioral problems in a large cross-sectional survey: Reliability and validity for children of the NLS youth.* Unpublished manuscript. Columbus, OH: Center for Human Resource Research, Ohio State University.

Pokropek, A., & Pokropek, E. (2022). Deep neural networks for detecting statistical model misspecifications: The case of measurement invariance. *Structural Equation Modeling, 29*, 394–411. https://doi.org/10.1080/10705511.2021.2010083.

Pokropek, A., Schmidt, P., & Davidov, E. (2020). Choosing priors in Bayesian measurement invariance modeling: A Monte Carlo simulation study. *Structural Equation Modeling, 27*, 750–764. https://doi.org/10.1080/10705511.2019.1703708.

Raftery, A. E. (1995). Bayesian model selection in social research. *Sociological Methodology*, *25*, 111–163. https://doi.org/10.2307/271063.

Raju, N., Fortmann-Johnson, K. A., Kim, W. et al. (2009). The item parameter replication method for detecting differential item functioning in the polytomous DFIT framework. *Applied Psychological Measurement*, *33*, 133–147. https://doi.org/10.1177/0146621608319514.

Raju, N.S. (1988). The area between two item characteristic curves. *Psychometrika 53*, 495–502. https://doi.org/10.1007/BF02294403.

Raju, N. S. (1990). Determining the significance of estimated signed and unsigned areas between two item response functions. *Applied Psychological Measurement*, *14*(2), 197–207. https://doi.org/10.1177/014662169001400208.

Rescorla, L. A., Adams, A., Ivanova, M. Y., & International ASEBA Consortium. (2020). The CBCL/1½–5's DSM-ASD scale: Confirmatory factor analyses across 24 societies. *Journal of Autism and Developmental Disorders*, *50*, 3326–3340. https://doi.org/10.1007/s10803-019-04189-5.

Rhemtulla, M., Brosseau-Liard, P. E., & Savalei, V. (2012). When can categorical variables be treated as continuous? A comparison of robust continuous and categorical SEM estimation methods under suboptimal conditions. *Psychological Methods*, *17*, 354–373. https://doi.org/10.1037/a0029315.

Rimfeld, K., Malanchini, M., Hannigan, L. J. et al. (2019). Teacher assessments during compulsory education are as reliable, stable and heritable as standardized test scores. *Journal of Child Psychology and Psychiatry*, *60*, 1278–1288. https://doi.org/10.1111/jcpp.13070.

Rious, J. B., Cunningham, M., & Spencer, M. B. (2019). Rethinking the notion of "hostility" in African American parenting styles. *Research in Human Development*, *16*, 35–50. https://doi.org/10.1080/15427609.2018.1541377.

Rotberg, I. C. (Ed.). (2010). *Balancing change and tradition in global education reform* (2nd ed.). Rowman & Littlefield.

Rothstein, M. G., & Goffin, R. D. (2006). The use of personality measures in personnel selection: What does current research support? *Human Resource Management Review*, *16*, 155–180. https://doi.org/10.1016/j.hrmr.2006.03.004.

Royston, P., Altman, D. G., & Sauerbrei, W. (2005). Dichotomizing continuous predictors in multiple regression: A bad idea. *Statistics in Medicine*, *25*, 127–141. https://doi.org/10.1002/sim.2331.

Sablan, J. R. (2019). Can you really measure that? Combining critical race theory and quantitative methods. *American Educational Research Journal*, *56*, 178–203. https://doi.org/10.3102/0002831218798325.

Samejima, F. (1969). *Estimation of ability using a response pattern of graded scores*. Psychometrika Monograph: No. 17. https://doi.org/10.1007/BF03372160.

Samejima, F. (1996). The graded response model. In W. J. van der Linden & R. K. Hambleton (Eds.), *Handbook of modern item response theory* (pp. 85–100). Springer. https://doi.org/10.1007/978-1-4757-2691-6_5.

Samejima, F. (2010). The general graded response model. In M. L. Nering & R. Ostini (Eds.), *Handbook of polytomous item response theory models* (pp. 77–107). Routledge.

Santori, D. (2020). *Test-based accountability in England*. Oxford Research Encyclopedias. Oxford University Press. https://doi.org/10.1093/acrefore/9780190264093.013.1454.

Seddig, D., & Lomazzi, V. (2019). Using cultural and structural indicators to explain measurement noninvariance in gender role attitudes with multilevel structural equation modeling. *Social Science Research*, *84*, 102328. https://doi.org/10.1016/j.ssresearch.2019.102328.

Sestir, M. A., Kennedy, L. A., Peszka, J. J., & Bartley, J. G. (2021). New statistics, old schools: An overview of current introductory undergraduate and graduate statistics pedagogy practices. *Teaching of Psychology*. https://doi.org/10.1177/00986283211030616.

Sharpe, D. (2013). Why the resistance to statistical innovations? Bridging the communication gap. *Psychological Methods*, *18*, 572–582. https://doi.org/10.1037/a0034177.

Shute, R. H., & Slee, P. T. (2015). *Child development theories and critical perspectives*. Routledge.

Sirganci, G., Uyumaz, G., & Yandi, A. (2020). Measurement invariance testing with alignment method: Many groups comparison. *International Journal of Assessment Tools in Education*, *7*, 657–673. https://doi.org/10.21449/ijate.714218.

Spencer, M. S., Fitch, D., Grogan-Taylor, A., & Mcbeath, B. (2005). The equivalence of the behavior problem index across U.S. ethnic groups. *Journal of Cross-Cultural Psychology*, *36*(5), 573–589. https://doi.org/10.1177/0022022105278

Sprague, J. (2016). *Feminist methodologies for critical researchers: Bridging differences*. Rowman & Littlefield.

Strobl, C., Kopf, J., Kohler, L., von Oertzen, T., & Zeileis, A. (2021). Anchor point selection: Scale alignment based on an inequality criterion. *Applied Psychological Measurement*, *45*, 214–230. https://doi.org/10.1177/0146621621990743.

Studts, C. R., Polaha, J., & van Zyl, M. A. (2017). Identifying unbiased items for screening preschoolers for disruptive behavior problems. *Journal of Pediatric Psychology*, *42*, 476–486. https://doi.org/10.1093/jpepsy/jsw090.

Svetina, D., Rutkowski, L., & Rutkowski, D. (2020). Multiple-group invariance with categorical outcomes using updated guidelines: An illustration using Mplus and the lavaan/semtools packages. *Structural Equation Modeling*, *27*, 111–130. https://doi.org/10.1080/10705511.2019.1602776.

Tay, L., Meade, A. W., & Cao, M. (2014). An overview and practice guide to IRT measurement equivalence analysis. *Organizational Research Methods*, *18*, 3–46. https://doi.org/10.1177/1094428114553062.

Walter, M., & Andersen, C. (2016). *Indigenous statistics: A quantitative research methodology*. Routledge. https://doi.org/10.4324/9781315426570.

Wen, C., & Hu, F. (2022). Investigating the applicability of alignment: A Monte Carlo simulation study. *Frontiers in Psychology*, *13*, 845721. https://doi.org/10.3389/fpsyg.2022.845721.

West, S. G., Taylor, A. B., & Wu, W. (2012). Model fit and model selection in structural equation modeling. In R. H. Hoyle (Ed.), *Handbook of structural equation modeling* (pp. 209–231). Guilford Press.

Winter, S. D., & Depaoli, S. (2020). An illustration of Bayesian approximate measurement invariance with longitudinal data and a small sample size. *International Journal of Behavioral Development*, *44*, 371–382. https://doi.org/10.1177/0165025419880610.

Wolfe, E. W., & Smith, E. V. (2007a). Instrument development tools and activities for measure validation using Rasch models: Part I – Instrument development tools. *Journal of Applied Measurement*, *8*, 97–123.

Wolfe, E. W., & Smith, E. V. (2007b). Instrument development tools and activities for measure validation using Rasch models: Part II – Validation activities. *Journal of Applied Measurement*, *8*, 204–234.

Woods C. M. (2009). Evaluation of MIMIC-model methods for DIF testing with comparison to two-group analysis. *Multivariate Behavioral Research*, *44*, 1–27. https://doi.org/10.1080/00273170802620121

Xi, X. (2010). How do we go about investigating test fairness? *Language Testing*, *27*, 147–170. https://doi.org/10.1177/0265532209349465.

Yoon, M., & Lai, M. H. C. (2018). Testing factorial invariance with unbalanced samples. *Structural Equation Modeling*, *25*, 201–213. https://doi.org/10.1080/10705511.2017.1387859.

Young, M. (2021, June 28). Down with meritocracy. *The Guardian: Politics*.

Zill, N. (1990). *Behavior problems index based on parent report.* Unpublished memo. Bethesda, MD: Child Trends.

Zlatkin-Troitschanskaia, O., Toepper, M., Pant, H. A., Lautenbach, C., & Kuhn, C. (Eds.). (2018). *Assessment of learning outcomes in higher education: Cross-national comparisons and perspectives.* Springer. https://doi.org/10.1007/978-3-319-74338-7.

Acknowledgment

Research reported in this publication was supported by the Eunice Kennedy Shriver National Institute of Child Health & Human Development of the National Institutes of Health under Award Number R03HD098310. The content is solely the responsibility of the authors and does not necessarily represent the official views of the National Institutes of Health. We gratefully acknowledge institutional support from the Institute for Health Research and Policy at the University of Illinois at Chicago and the Center for Advanced Studies in Measurement and Assessment at the University of Iowa. Data and code used for this manuscript are available through supplementary materials. The Harmony R package is available through GitHub. This study's design and its analysis were not pre-registered.

Cambridge Elements $\equiv$

Research Methods for Developmental Science

Brett Laursen
Florida Atlantic University

Brett Laursen is a Professor of Psychology at Florida Atlantic University. He is Editor-in-Chief of the *International Journal of Behavioral Development*, where he previously served as the founding Editor of the Methods and Measures section. Professor Laursen received his Ph.D. in Child Psychology from the Institute of Child Development at the University of Minnesota and an Honorary Doctorate from Örebro University, Sweden. He is a Docent Professor of Educational Psychology at the University of Helsinki, and a Fellow of the American Psychological Association (Division 7, Developmental), the Association for Psychological Science, and the International Society for the Study of Behavioural Development. Professor Laursen is the co-editor of the *Handbook of Developmental Research Methods* and the *Handbook of Peer Interactions, Relationships, and Groups*.

About the Series

Each offering in this series will focus on methodological innovations and contemporary strategies to assess adjustment and measure change, empowering scholars of developmental science who seek to optimally match their research questions to pioneering methods and quantitative analyses.

Cambridge Elements ≡

Research Methods for Developmental Science

Printed in the United States
by Baker & Taylor Publisher Services